Top 25 locator map
(continues on inside
back cover)

KT-155-729

TwinPack
Cyprus

ROBERT BULMER

Robert Bulmer lived for
many years in Cyprus. He
returns often, to walk in the
hills, explore again the towns
and villages or simply
luxuriate on the beaches.
His book, *Days Out in
Cyprus*, published by
himself, was followed by the
AA's *Essential Cyprus* and
then by AA Thomas Cook
Travellers Cyprus.

If you have any comments
or suggestions for this guide
you can contact the editor at
Twinpacks@theAA.com

AA Publishing
Find out more about AA Publishing and the
wide range of travel publications and
services the AA provides by visiting our
website at *www.theAA.com/bookshop*

Contents

life 5–12

how to organise your time 13–22

top 25 sights 23–48

Index 92–93

About this book

KEY TO SYMBOLS

✚ Grid reference to the
   Top 25 locator map

✉ Address

☎ Telephone number

🕐 Opening times

🍴 Restaurant or café on premises
   or near by

Ⓜ Nearest underground (tube)
   station

🚉 Nearest railway station

🚌 Nearest bus route

⛴ Nearest riverboat or ferry stop

♿ Facilities for visitors with
   disabilities

✋ Admission charge

↔ Other nearby places of interest

❓ Tours, lectures or special events

▶ Indicates the page where you
   will find a fuller description

ℹ Tourist information

TwinPack Cyprus is divided into six sections to cover the six most important aspects of your visit to Cyprus. It includes:

- The author's view of the island and its people
- Suggested walks and excursions
- The Top 25 Sights to visit
- The best of the rest – aspects of the island that make it special
- Detailed listings of restaurants, hotels, shops and nightlife
- Practical information

In addition, easy-to-read side panels provide fascinating extra facts and snippets, highlights of places to visit and invaluable practical advice.

CROSS-REFERENCES
To help you make the most of your visit, cross-references, indicated by ▶, show you where to find additional information about a place or subject.

MAPS
The fold-out map in the wallet at the back of the book is a large-scale island map of Cyprus.
The Top 25 locator maps found on the inside front and back covers of the book itself are for quick reference. They show the Top 25 Sights, described on pages 24–48, which are clearly plotted by number (**1**–**25**, not page number) in alphabetical order.

PRICES
Where appropriate, an indication of the cost of an establishment is given by £ signs: £££ denotes higher prices, ££ denotes average prices, while £ denotes lower charges.

CYPRUS
life

A Personal View

Eating out in Cyprus is literally that, alfresco, and there is something immensely satisfying in dining under the stars in the cool of the evening to a background chorus of *cicadas*. It suits everybody; the restauranteur saves the expense of elaborate premises and interior décor, the clientele find it a marvellous experience. On top of that the waiters and waitresses really look as if they are having as much fun as the customers.

Priest at Asinou Church

Few travellers are able to take the advice of the celebrated author Lawrence Durrell and make landfall at Cyprus from the sea. Nevertheless, the normally more mundane alternative of an air passage has its compensations. For a start, the first taste of Cyprus will be taken early for on a Cyprus Airways flight it starts at the airport check in. The animated Greek conversation, a fascinating aural amalgam of deltas, thetas, epsilons and omegas, of Greek Cypriots homeward bound, straining at hand baggage too heavy to lift, confirms as clearly as any marker board that the destination is Cyprus.

The memories come flooding back and even more so in the clear air over western Cyprus. Any expert of the island, window seat permitting, is duty bound to identify as many landmarks as possible. Pafos town, old and new, is of course easy and keen eyes may pick out the Tombs of the Kings, the Roman amphitheatre beside the lighthouse and, further down the coast, the ancient site of Palea Pafos. From the skies the summer landscape appears impressively arid and parched with only a little indication of the colourful splendours portrayed in tourist publications. The reason of course is simple: Cyprus is the hottest of the Mediterranean islands and throughout the long summer receives not one drop of rain.

The heat may not strike one 'as a drawn sword' as another Lawrence (TE) famously said of Arabia but at midday it is not to be underestimated. Unacclimatised visitors are wise if they wait for longer shadows before exploring the towns and villages or venturing into the ancient ruins. And when the sun is at its zenith the beaches are best left to mad dogs and tanned masochists.

The big consolation is that hot sun and perspiration can add an extra dimension to the Cyprus experience. Salamis and Kourion in spring may be wonderful but are as nothing compared with a midsummer expedition through their archaeological magnificence. The searing heat leaves the brain fit only to contemplate the immediate surroundings and to imagine, if only a little, what these ruined and deserted cities might have been like at the height of their power and authority.

Cooler weather returns for late September or October and with the winter rains the land is transformed into a luxuriant green. In April the justifiably famous Cyprus spring sees the vast coastal Mesaorian plain become a blaze of colour, the wild flowers are magnificent and the smell of citrus blossom is everywhere.

Cyprus is an island undergoing relentless change. In just a few years the country's wealth has grown dramatically. In 2004 the Greek Cypriot population joined the European Union. Enthusiasm for Europe is such that long-familiar place names have been changed at some cost to comply with obscure Brussels inspired directives regarding phonetic spelling.

Perhaps the pace of development will slow. Maybe the wonderful Akamas peninsula will remain unspoilt and the Karpas a place of one car an hour. Possibly the massive stones of distant, forgotten ancient Aphendrika will lie undisturbed in the long grasses. It does not seem likely; once every Cypriot household aspired to own a long Mercedes saloon, now it is a wide off-roader with the potential to traverse any stony and improbable track. It is doubtful if any Cypriot could begin to comprehend that many lovers of Cyprus are not enthusiastically awaiting the day when the island might cast off its unique individuality straddling the cultures of east and west.

LINGUISTICS OF EXCESS

A stranger to Cyprus might imagine that every Cypriot speaks English, such are the linguistic skills of the populace. This widespread fluency presents opportunities that are unavailable in destinations where phrase books and sign language promote verbal incomprehension.

Nevertheless it is English with a slightly different rule book and even more so after a double Cyprus brandy, but it is certainly entertaining. And if the Cypriots have mastered languages they have mastered the art of eastern hospitality even more so. There is an impressive willingness, if not compulsion, to feed guests beyond physical endurance and to which there is no polite defence or escape.

Locals meet in Polis

Cyprus in Figures

GEOGRAPHY
- The island has two significant mountain ranges. Troodos in the centre reaches 1,951m, high enough to ensure snow cover in winter; the Kyrenia range, at 1,046m, is in the Turkish-controlled sector of the island.
- There are approximately 3,350 hours of sunshine a year, with little chance of rain between May and October.
- Sheep cope with the shortage of grazing in the summer by storing fat in their tails.

PEOPLE
- The first sign of human habitation dates from 11,000 years ago.
- Population is 895,000 of whom about 705,000 are Greek Cypriots, 160,000 Turkish Cypriots, 8,000 Armenians and Maronites. The rest are foreigners.
- The Cypriots have the highest marriage rate in Europe.

TOURISM
- The island attracts about 2.75 million visitors a year and tourism provides employment for some 37,000 people or 13 per cent of the workforce, many of them immigrants.

ECONOMIC FACTORS
- Forty-six per cent of the land area is cultivated, the main crops being cereals, potatoes and citrus fruits.
- Cyprus has the third highest standard of living in the Mediterranean. The average income here is twice as high as it is in Greece.
- In the past Cyprus suffered water shortages because of dry winters. Four desalination plants have been constructed, providing some 120,000 cu m of water each day.

CLIMATE EXTREMES
- Cyprus in summer is a hot place, certainly the hottest of the Mediterranean islands, and, of course, sun worshippers love it. It is difficult to imagine that winter days can be cool and wet with snow falling on the highest ground, creating a winter wonderland among the pine trees.

People of Cyprus

Makarios

Archbishop Makarios was the first president of Cyprus. He remains a Greek Cypriot national hero and there are statues of him all around the island. He was born in 1913 and became a priest at Kykkos Monastery. After a period working in Greece and the United States, he was appointed bishop of Pafos and later archbishop of the whole island. He soon became part of the highly politicised world of the Cypriot Church and their campaign for *Enosis*, or Union, with Greece and against the British. In 1956, as a result of these activities, he was deported to the Seychelles. A year later he was freed but was not allowed to return to Cyprus. It was from Athens, therefore, that he began the final negotiations for independence, having abandoned *Enosis*, and in February 1959 a deal was signed. Independence was achieved in August 1960.

Makarios then became president, but inter-communal strife soon emerged and the United Nations had to keep the peace. Tensions continued to grow and in 1974 Makarios was deposed in a Greek-sponsored military coup. Makarios escaped, but Turkey invaded and the island was divided. He returned and ruled for another three years before his death in 1977, ushering in a new secular era in Cypriot politics.

Richard the Lionheart

King Richard I of England came to Cyprus on his way to the Crusades and changed the course of the island's history. Part of his fleet was shipwrecked in 1191, including the ship carrying his sister and his fiancée, Berengaria. The ruler of Cyprus, Isaac Comnenos, treated them badly and Richard retaliated, having first married Berengaria in St George's Chapel, Limassol. After a month of battles Comnenos surrendered and Richard took control of the island. However, he was not enamoured with his conquest and, fearing it would be more trouble than it was worth, arranged to pass it on to Guy de Lusignan, a French knight. This ushered in a 300-year rule by the Lusignan dynasty.

VISITORS TO CYPRUS

Few native Cypriots have achieved international celebrity but the island has attracted illustrious visitors throughout its history. Island mythology claims the birth of Aphrodite and visits from a succession of Greek gods. Christian influences were brought by St Paul, St Barnabas and St Lazarus and literary visitors have included the French poet Rimbaud, and British authors Lawrence Durrell and Colin Thubron. More recently, as a sign of its status as a world troublespot, a succession of international statesman have been despatched here in attempts to solve the 'Cyprus Problem'.

Archbishop Makarios, the island's first president and a national hero to Greek Cypriots

A Chronology

9000–3800 BC	First migrants arrive from Asia Minor. Neolithic settlements built at Choirokoitia and Cape Apostolos Andreas.
3800–2500 BC	Chalcolithic period. Erimi and Lemba became important centres of habitation.
2500–1050 BC	Bronze Age settlers arrive from the eastern Mediterranean. Alambra and Nitovikla the principal locations.
700 BC	Assyria claims control of Cyprus.
570 BC	Egyptian pharaoh Amasis becomes effective ruler of Cyprus.
545 BC	Cyprus submits to King Cyrus of Persia. Two hundred years of Persian rule follow.
325–50 BC	Hellenistic period: Cyprus becomes part of the Greek world. The people adopt Greek dress and Greek architectural styles are imitated.
50 BC–AD 330	Roman rule and the building of great amphitheatres, baths and temples.
AD 45	Evangelising visit of St Paul; said to have converted the Roman governor to Christianity.
330–395	Split in Roman Empire and the start of the Byzantine era.
7th and 10th centuries	Arab raids.
1191	Richard the Lionheart, en route to the Holy Land, conquers Cyprus and marries Princess Berengaria in Limassol.
1192–1489	Lusignan Rule. The great Latin cathedrals of Nicosia and Famagusta are built.
1489	Venetians, invited to help against troublesome Genoese in Famagusta, take the island for themselves.
1571	Ottoman Turks subjugate Cyprus.

1878	Britain, in agreement with Turkey, takes control of the island.
1914	Britain formally annexes Cyprus as a consequence of Turkey fighting for Germany in World War I.
1955	EOKA (Ethniki Organosis Kyprion Agoniston, or the National Organisation of Cypriot Fighters), under Grivas, begins a guerrilla campaign in order to unite Cyprus with Greece.
1960	Cyprus granted Independence. Archbishop Makarios III becomes president.
1963	Inter-communal fighting. Turks retreat into enclaves.
1974	Military coup against Makarios, who flees the island. Five days later Turkish forces invade and soon take control of north Cyprus. Rauf Denktash appointed leader in the north. Makarios returns to south Cyprus.
1975	Nicosia airport remains under United Nations control. Greek Cypriots build airport at Larnaka and begin to revive tourism.
1977	Makarios dies and is succeeded as president by Spirou Kyprianou.
1983	Turks unilaterally proclaim Turkish Republic of Northern Cyprus.
1984	UN-sponsored talks end in a stalemate.
1996	Trouble flares on the buffer zone bewteen the communities; two Greek Cypriots are killed.
2003	First time in nearly 30 years Greek and Turkish Cypriots are allowed across the Green Line.
2004	UN referendum for reunification. Turkish Cypriots vote for the plan, Greek Cypriots overwhemingly against. Greek Cypriot controlled part of the island joins the EU.

11

Best of Cyprus

A Greek wedding at the ancient theatre in Kourion

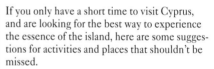

If you only have a short time to visit Cyprus, and are looking for the best way to experience the essence of the island, here are some suggestions for activities and places that shouldn't be missed.

- Go to the Roman theatre at Kourion (► 30) for a classical drama: the atmosphere is electric. They are held regularly throughout the summer – details from the tourist office.

- Find a quiet beach, preferably fringed with bushes or tall grasses, and take a swim before breakfast.

- Have a drink in a village coffee shop. Be prepared to be ignored, but it is much more likely that someone will chance their English and start a conversation.

- Join a plate-breaking session in a Greek tavern. This mayhem is not as common as it once was, but local enquiries may lead to a venue.

- Ski or toboggan on Mount Olympus. No chance here for summer visitors, the season is from 1st January to the end of March.

- Have a full *meze* alfresco style off the tourist track. Be prepared to stay awake all night with a distended stomach.

- Drive to Petra tou Romiou, or Rock of Romios (► 44) in the late afternoon and stop on the clifftop a little to the east. The view is tremendous.

- Join in a Greek dance. The impressiveness of the steps is hardly matched by the difficulty. Take a couple of brandy sours first.

Petra tou Romiou

- Walk a forest trail in the Troodos or Kyrenia Mountains until perspiring freely, then sit down and have a picnic.

CYPRUS
how to organise
your time

A Walk Around Larnaka

The walk starts at the northern end of the seafront by the marina.

Head inland on Pavlou Street, passing the tourist office before turning left into Zinonos Kitieos Street. This is the main shopping street of Larnaka. It also contains the Pierides Museum, which houses an enormous and highly varied range of historical artefacts from all over Cyprus (➤ 50).

Pass the yellow building of the Armenian Church and later the municipal market at the corner of Ermou Street. There is a very confusing maze of intersections at the end of Zinonos Kitieos Street requiring a sharp right and then follow the road round to the left.

The old mosque which is passed is now a youth hostel in the Laiki Geitonia. A little further (about five minutes) is Agios Lazaros Church (➤ 51).

After exploring the church and its graveyard, head back towards the seafront down Agiou Lazarou Street.

This was once the Turkish part of town and the minaret of Djami Kebir mosque can be seen. Although it is still used by visiting Muslims, it is open to the public when services are not taking place.

Follow the main road back to the shore, and Larnaka fort is to the right. It is worth pausing for a moment to take in the view from the south of the fort, where the coastline stretches away in a long strip of tourist development.

It is a straight walk along the seafront, or along the beach, back to the marina.

INFORMATION

Distance 2km
Time 1–2 hours
Start/end point The Marina, Larnaka
🚌 18
🍴 Old Mansion, Archontiko (£)
✉ 24 Athinon Avenue
☎ 2465 5905

The campanile of Agios Lazaros Church

A Limassol Walk

This walk starts on the seafront by the car parks and sculpture park. Follow the promenade southwest to a small roundabout which marks the old harbour, complete with fishing boats. There is a small reptile house on one corner with a collection of local and foreign species.

Proceed inland to the 14th-century Castle and Medieval Museum (► 54). Turn right along Genthliou Mitella Street and pass a mosque which is still in use.

This was once the Turkish part of the town and many of the older houses are of a typical Turkish design. The municipal fruit and vegetable market lies just east of the mosque.

Continue northeast until the road leads into Agiou Andreou Street, the main shopping street.

There are many narrow alleyways in this area, but they are interesting to explore and walkers should not worry about getting lost as they will eventually emerge on to the wider thoroughfare. Agiou Andreou has a wide range of shops, from the usual souvenirs to leather goods and jewellery.

After about 1km Agia Trias Church can be visited a short way up Agias Triados Street, just before Zinonos Street. Returning to the main road the Folk Art Museum is found a little way on, and to the left. One kilometre farther along Agiou Andreou Street, at the north side of the municipal gardens, turn right on Kanningkos Street to reach the Archaeological Museum, 200m to the left. The walk ends in the municipal gardens, which offer relief from the busy city streets.

INFORMATION

Distance 2.5km
Time 1–3½ hours
Start point Seafront car park, Limassol
End point Municipal gardens
🍴 Cafés opposite the castle (£)
✉ Eirinis Street

Street scene, Limossol

A Walk Around Pafos

INFORMATION

Distance 3.5km
Time 1–4 hours
Start/end point Pafos harbour
🚌 10, 15 to Coral Bay
🍴 Several cafés along the harbour (££)

The walk begins at the fenced-off World Heritage Site by the harbour and the first section of the route is thorugh the archaeological ruins. There is a modest charge to enter but it includes access to the famous mosaics (➤ 43), Odeion (➤ 53), Saranda Kolones (➤ 54) and other antiquities.

Follow the pavement to the mosaics which are among the most impressive in the world. From here the walk is to the Odeion, a restored Roman theatre dating from the 2nd century AD, a good marker being the prominent lighthouse adjacent to it.

Pafos lighthouse above the ancient ruins

From this elevated gound there are excellent views and Saranda Kolones is visible to the south-east. It is a detour and perhaps better saved for another day.

The direct route is generally east, carefully following the signs from Apostolou Pavlou Avenue. At the avenue turn left and about 250m farther on the right-hand side is the catacomb of Agia Solomoni.

The church is marked by a tree covered in handkerchiefs and is in the furthest cave.

Return down Apostolou Pavlou Avenue for about 400m, turn left into Stilis Agiou Pavlou Street to reach the site of St Paul's Pillar after about 200m.

The pillar is the site where St Paul was whipped on the order of the Romans (➤ 59). Adjacent to the pillar is the church of Agia Kyriaki.

Return to Apostolou Pavlou Avenue, turn left and you'll reach the harbour after 500m.

A Famagusta Walk

The walk starts at the Land Gate entrance of the historic walled city.

Istiklal Caddesi is directly opposite and should be followed, taking care not to lose it at the three-way junction after 130m. About 130m further, on the left, is the Church of SS Peter and Paul, now a public library.

A right turn along Sinan Paşa Sokagi leads to the Palazzo de Proveditore (Venetian Palace). From here it is a small distance to Namik Kemal Zindani (Square), overlooked by the magnificent west front of Lala Mustafa Paşa Mosque (▶ 34).

A short retreat (to the west) picks up Kisla Sokagi, and in 130m are the twin churches (now restored) of the Knights Templar and Knights Hospitaller. Immediately beyond the churches the road turns right, to the northeast, and in 120m Cafer Paşa Sokagi.

At the eastern end stand the ruined, but impressive, buttresses and lancet windows of St George of the Latins. The Citadel (Othello's Tower) is a short distance to the north and should not be bypassed.

The walk continues alongside the sea wall, down Canbulat Yolu, to reach the splendid Sea Gate after 200m.

In another 160m a short detour along M Ersu Sokagi brings walkers to the substantial Church of St George of the Greeks. Returning to the main road, the Canbulat Museum is reached in 300m.

The return to the Land Gate is about 1100m. Pass outside the walls at the Canbulat Museum and follow the south wall.

INFORMATION

Distance 2.75km
Time 1–3½ hours
Start/end point Land Gate, Famagusta
🍴 Café opposite west front of Lala Mustafa Paşa Mosque (£)

Land Gate and Ravelin, scenes of desperate fighting in the great siege of 1570-71

A Drive from Limassol to Petra tou Romiou

INFORMATION

Distance 65km
Time 1½–5 hours
Start point Limassol town centre
End point Petra tou Romiou
🍴 Bunch of Grapes (££)
✉ Pissouri Village
☎ 25221275

The stadium at Kourion

The drive begins in Limassol town centre. Head towards the new port, then turn west to Asomatos and Fassouri, passing through citrus groves.

The dense citrus groves around the village provide a pleasant drive, and guided tours are also available.

Turn north to Kolossi Castle, a seat of the Knights Hospitallers (➤ 29). After Kolossi village turn left and in 2km the road passes through the village of Episkopi.

This village was founded in the 7th century by refugees from Kourion. More recently it has become home to British services personnel and their families from the nearby British base. From the village it is a short detour to the site of Kourion (➤ 30), the most impressive archaeological site in the south of the island.

Rejoin the main road, taking great care on the dangerous bends, and continue towards Pafos.

In about 1km, on the inland side of the road, is Kourion Stadium and after a further 2km is the Temple of Apollo Hylates, another very impressive place (➤ 53). Immediately beyond this the road enters the British base of Episkopi to start a steep descent to the green playing fields of Happy Valley. These are a striking contrast to their dusty surroundings.

To the west of the base is a turning to splendid Avdimou Beach (➤ 55), some 3km away on a very narrow, although metalled track. The main route continues along the coast. Pissouri, a few kilometres further, provides an alternative beach and the possibility of lunch in the village. Beyond here the route runs high in the cliffs, with some really spectacular scenery, but on a slow road.

Continue for another 6km to reach Petra tou Romiou, the legendary birthplace of Aphrodite.

A Drive from Kyrenia to Kantara

The outward leg of this drive has few route-finding problems, staying close to the magnificent shore most of the way.

Drivers should take the coast road east out of Kyrenia, towards Agios Epiktitos (Çatalköy). In colonial days the British put down mile posts and all beaches of significance on this north shore were described by the distance to Kyrenia. Six Mile Beach (also Acapulco), Eight Mile Beach and Twelve Mile Beach are all on the route. The latter is the longest sandy stretch on the coast, but it cannot be seen from the road. The villages of Karaagac, Esentepe, Bahceli and Tatlisu are all 2 or 3km off the main route. A detour to Tatlisu is recommended.

From the Tatlisu junction it is another 19km to reach the south turn to Kaplica. Now the road climbs steeply up to the village of Kantara.

Its castle (► 54), another 6km along the mountain ridge, is certainly worth visiting. Return to the village before starting the rapid descent to Turnalar, Yarkoy and on to the pleasant village of Bogaz, overlooking the Bay of Famagusta. The return section of the drive is southwest for 4km, before turning west to Iskele, the birthplace of the EOKA leader. Grivas. Gecitkale, a large village in a parched landscape in summer, is another 19km away.

A narrow road runs west, and after about 16km follow Lefkosa (Nicosia) signs to reach the main highway. After 12km, turn right for Girne (Kyrenia) to ascend rapidly to the pass at 750m above sea level, with Besparmak Mountain looming large to the right.

Now it is all downhill towards the sea, with another 12km along the coast to Kyrenia to take a well-earned driving rest at a harbourside café.

INFORMATION

Distance 190km
Time 4½–7½ hours
Start/end point Kyrenia
🍴 Cafés in Kantara village (£)

Along the scenic coast towards Kantara

Finding Peace & Quiet

Despite the popularity of Cyprus' resorts there are still many places on the island to escape the crowds and find a little peace and quiet.

AKAMAS' GORGES

A few companies, including Exalt Travel of Pafos (☎ 2694 3803), offer guided tours through the gorges, the Avgas being the favourite. It is something of an adventure, negotiating the boulder-strewn river bed with high sheer cliffs on either side. If the weather is, or is likely to be, bad the gorges should be avoided – flash floods here can be extremely dangerous.

AVDIMOU GORGE
Drive to Avdimou beach (► 55) about 30km west of Limassol. but select the gravel track to Melanda Tavern not the road to Avdimou Jetty to the east. The beach itself is often deserted but the cliff-top path running west is a delight, with wonderful views over the coastal strip, and eventually reaching the high cliffs above Pisouri beach. There is, however, no necessity to go more than 200m to find solitude. Occasionally the RAF perform manoeuvres just offshore, not very peaceful but spectacular.

CEDAR VALLEY
This is best reached from Pafos, Pano Panagia being the last outpost before setting out on the unmetalled track into the western forest. The valley is 12km away, a good map is needed and an all-terrain vehicle is best for the uncertainties ahead. At 400m above sea level, under the canopy of trees, the air is cool. The cedars are magnificent and the stillness of the forest is only likely to be disturbed by the crashing of a moufflon (wild mountain sheep) taking fright, or the trickle of water from a perennial spring.

FAMAGUSTA BAY
The stretch of coast starting about 9km north of Protaras offers some fine clifftop walks. Access is not entirely obvious. Once on the low escarpments all is straightforward, including a view of the abandoned, crumbling Varosha suburb of Famagusta (► 26) – take binoculars.

KARPASIA
Much of northern Cyprus is quiet, but the Karpasia is even quieter, with only the local population going about their business. You should take a map and simply set off on a journey of exploration stopping at any beach, ancient site or village that attracts their attention.

Western forest en route to the fabled cedars

MANDRIA SHORE

Turn into Mandria village, east of the road to Pafos airport. Follow the beach signs to Pasa church and after 500m you will reach a T-junction. Go left for another 500m and turn right to reach the shore after 1km, with its pleasant shingle beach.

PETOUNDA POINT

Take the road west of Kiti village towards Petounda Point for about 6km. Turn left at the sign for Panagia Petounda church and after about 1.5km you'll see the church on the right, but keep left. There are two houses, but a short walk to the west brings isolation.

POMOS POINT TO KATO PYRGOS

This section of coast, northeast of Polis in the west, sees fewer visitors than most others in southern Cyprus, although nothing is guaranteed. Several stretches of dark sand line the

SHY MOUFFLON

The adverse fortune in recent years of one of Cyprus' oldest, shyest and most distinctive residents is now over. The moufflon, the largest wild animal in Cyprus, was declared a protected species in 1995. This deliverance was timely – the numbers of the impressive horned sheep had been reduced to just 300 by relentless hunting.

varied bays and coves. The further east the quieter it is. Here the Troodos Mountains descend dramatically to the sea. In the event of a sudden influx of tourist buses there is the opportunity to retreat quickly into the quiet hills and gaze down on the coast from a good height.

Secluded beaches near Pomos Point

21

What's On

JANUARY	*New Year's Day* (1 Jan)
	Epiphany (6 Jan): one of the most important Greek Orthodox religious celebrations of the year
MARCH	*Greek National Day* (25 Mar): parades and celebrations
APRIL	*National Day* (1 Apr): anniversary of the EOKA uprising
	Turkish Children's Festival (23 Apr)
MAY	*Labour Day* (1 May)
	May Fair in Pafos (1 May): 10 days of cultural events and exhibitions of Cypriot flora, basket-work and embroidery
	Anthestiria Flower Festivals (early May): the festivals' origins go back to celebrations honouring the god Dionysos in Ancient Greece
	Turkish Youth Festival (19 May)
	Cyprus International Fair (late May): the largest trade fair in Cyprus, held in Nicosia and lasting 10 days
JULY	*Larnaka Festival* (throughout Jul): performances of dance and theatre in the fort and the Pattichon amphitheatre
AUGUST/SEPTEMBER	*Turkish Communal Resistance Day* (1 Aug)
	Turkish Victory Day (30 Aug)
	Limassol Wine Festival (late Aug–first week in Sep): a 12-day indulgence of free wine, with music and dance some evenings
OCTOBER	*Independence Day* (1 Oct)
	Greek National Day (28 Oct): also known as Ochi Day. Student parades all over southern Cyprus
	Turkish National Day (29 Oct)
NOVEMBER	*Proclamation of Turkish Republic of North Cyprus* (15 Nov)
DECEMBER	*Christmas Day* (25 Dec)

Traditional dancers at a festival in Agia Napa

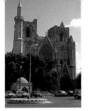

CYPRUS'
top 25 sights

The sights are shown on the maps on the inside front cover and inside back cover, numbered **1**–**25** alphabetically

Akamas

1

INFORMATION

➕ A3
✉ Cyprus' westernmost land
🍴 Baths of Aphrodite Tourist
   Pavilion Café (££)
❓ Across the road from the
   café is a pool called The
   Baths of Aphrodite

A beautiful region of hills, valleys and rocky shores, Akamas is ideal for rambling, with rich and varied flora and diverse wildlife habitats.

This westernmost extremity of Cyprus is unique in the Greek part of the island, not only for its beauty but also for the absence of tourist development. This can be explained partly by its remoteness, and by a British military firing range, Three areas are now designated protected and no development is permitted.

The vegetation is Mediterranean, with large tracts of impenetrable maquis interspersed with a thin covering of pine trees and juniper. Autumn-flowering cyclamen are everywhere. In places the landscape is impressively stark with spectacular rock outcrops. On the beaches green and loggerhead turtles still come up to lay their eggs, and occasionally a monk seal may be sighted.

The magnificent and unspoiled Akamas coast

Although there are no metalled roads, the area is becoming popular with motorcyclists and ramblers. Several walking trails have been created, starting by the Baths of Aphrodite, west of Polis. A network of marked paths traverses the hills and information panels describe the types of flora. These are described in a free booklet from the tourist office called *Nature Trails of the Akamas*. The ascent of Mouti tis Sotiras is worth contemplating – it only takes an hour to reach the summit and the view is surely the best in Greek Cyprus. Needless to say, in summer it is a hot and sticky expedition. An alternative is to take a boat from Latsi (Lakkí) for a swim and a picnic in one of the delightful coves, perhaps near Fontana Amoroza (Love's Spring), halfway to Cape Arnaoutis.

Bellapais Abbey

The location of the abbey on the northern slopes of the Kyrenia Mountains is marvellous. Far below are the almond and olive groves of the coastal plain.

Augustinian canons founded the abbey at the end of the 12th century and its importance lasted for some 300 years. Substantial parts collapsed long ago; the cloister is partly ruined, window tracery hangs down from the pointed arches.

On the north side is the Refectory, where the vaults of the roof appear to spring lightly from their capitals. Six tall windows look out on to the northern shore, and an exquisite pulpit, reached by an intricate stair, is ingeniously built into the thickness of the wall.

The 13th-century church is generally locked, but the custodian may open it on request.

In 1995 forest fires swept through the Kyrenia Mountains, swiftly advancing on Beylerbeyi, the village where the author Lawrence Durrell lived from 1953–56. The fires lived up to Durrell's description in his celebrated book *Bitter Lemons* where he wrote 'two things spread quickly: gossip and a forest fire'. It was only good fortune and the skill of the fire-fighters that prevented the destruction of Beylerbeyi in July 1995.

INFORMATION

➕ C2

✉ Bellapais (Beylerbeyi) village

🕐 Jun–Sep, daily 9–7; Oct–May, daily 9–1, 2–4:45 💲 Moderate

🍴 Café at the gate (£)

The church, the oldest and best-preserved part of the abbey, is occasionally used for services

25

Famagusta (Gazimağusa)

INFORMATION

✚ E2

🏠 Fevzi Cakmak Bulvari

☎ 366 2864

🍴 Cafés widespread (£–££)

Before delving into its medieval history, view the forbidden city of Famagusta from the cliff-tops of Famagusta Bay.

The city is divided. Varosha, the new town, with its painted hotels bordering the sandy beach, is closed to all but the military. Visitors must therefore concentrate on the walled city – one of the finest surviving examples of medieval military architecture.

To pass through the massive walls is to pass through history, from the time of the Lusignans, Genoese and Venetians to the bloody siege by the Turks in 1570–71. They stormed the walls and all Cyprus was theirs for over 300 years, and the scene was set for the troubles of today.

In the narrow streets the shops are unchanged by time or fashion. Dark interiors hide a miscellany of goods. The town can be a bustling place of noise and activity, but more often it is calm, the residents going about their business in a relaxed manner. They may not be as outgoing as the Greek Cypriots in the south, but they are equally courteous and helpful.

Famagusta beach

There is much unexpected open space in all directions; a chaotic panorama of unkempt gardens and scrubland where palm trees shade ancient domed churches. Splendid crumbling examples of medieval buildings are all around. The battered minaret and massive buttress of Lala Mustafa Paşa mosque are an impressive landmark for any who get lost in these exotic surroundings.

Famagusta's Venetian Walls

The original plan of the town was laid out by the Lusignans but when the Venetians took over in 1489 they completely renovated the boundary walls.

Experts in military architecture, the Venetians lowered the ramparts but increased the thickness, taking out all features that were vulnerable to cannon fire.

Any tour of the fortifications should take into account the great heat of summer and the unguarded parapets everywhere. The Citadel should be visited. It is also known as Othello's Tower, a name derived from Shakespeare's play, set in a 'seaport in Cyprus'. Four great cylindrical towers guard the corners of the Citadel. Over the entrance the carving is of an impressive winged lion of St Mark. The great hall is a massive vaulted chamber. Taking a clockwise circuit of the walls, the Sea Gate, 200m southeast, is the next place of interest. The gate's portcullis is part of the original Venetian installation. In another 500m is the Canbulat Gate and bastion (Canbulat was a Turkish hero of the siege), now a museum. Muskets and swords are displayed next to period dresses finished with fine embroidery. Three bastions on the southern wall lead to the Land Gate, the main entrance to the town. It is part of the Ravelin, a bastion considered impregnable when built, but later found wanting as its ditch offered cover to the enemy.

INFORMATION

✚ e6
🕐 Citadel and museum:
Jun–Sep, Mon–Fri 10–5
(museum Jun–Sep
Mon–Fri 9–5); Oct–May,
Mon–Fri 9–1, 2–4:45.
Elsewhere no restrictions
♿ Citadel and museum,
moderate
🍴 Cafés nearby (£)

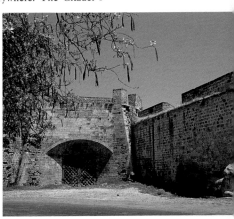

Looking up to the Venetian Walls

Hala Sultan Tekke & Larnaka Salt Lake

INFORMATION

✚ D3

✉ 3km west of Larnaka on the Kition road

🕐 Jun–Aug, daily 7:30–7:30; Sep–May, daily 9–5

🎫 Free, but donation requested

🚌 Bus from Larnaka; drop-off on the main road

↔ Kiti church (Panagia Angeloktistos, ▶ 51)

A Muslim holy shrine standing on the shore of a spectacular natural landmark which has very different aspects in winter and summer.

The Hala Sultan Tekke's importance is surpassed only by the shrines of Mecca, Medina and al Aksha (Jerusalem). It was here that the prophet Mohammed's maternal aunt, Umm Haram, was buried in AD 649. Apparently, she fell from a donkey and broke her neck while participating in an Arab raid on the island. Three enormous stones were raised to mark her grave and thereafter the site became an important place of pilgrimage for Muslims. The mosque, with its distinctive dome and minaret, was built by the Turks in 1816, although the tomb was built in 1760. Visitors are permitted to enter the mosque but must respect the dress code and remove their shoes before entering.

In the summer the surrounding gardens with their impressive palm trees are a relatively cool haven from the blistering heat of the Salt Lake. This is a desert for much of the year, but in winter the lake fills with water and attracts a wide range of migrating birds. In summer the water evaporates, leaving a dusty grey expanse which shimmers in the heat. The salt used to be a significant product in the island's economy, but today it is no longer economically viable to collect it. It originates from the nearby sea, seeping up through the porous rocks during the rainy months.

The most spectacular of the winter visitors are the distinctive pink flamingos.

Hala Sultan Tekke is an important Islamic shrine

Kolossi Castle

Kolossi was the headquarters of the Knights Hospitallers, who probably built the first fortress in the late 13th century.

The Knights Hospitallers exploited the area, using locally produced sugar and grapes to make Commandaria wine.

The castle suffered from a number of attacks by Egyptian Mameluke raiders in the 14th century, and the buildings visible today date from rebuilding which took place in the 15th century. The Turks took it over in 1570 and sugar production continued until 1799.

Visitors pass over a drawbridge into a pleasant garden and then into the keep, which has walls 2.75m thick and is three storeys (23m) high. The defenders used to throw boiling oil from the parapet on to the attackers below.

Much of the ground floor was used as a storage area. The first floor has two large rooms and a kitchen. On the second floor were the apartments of the Grand Commander, which have an airy feel to them created by four large windows. A spiral staircase leads to the roof, from where there are good views. The large vaulted building in the grounds was the place where the sugar was made.

INFORMATION

- C4
- 14.5km from Limassol
- 2593 4907
- Jun–Aug, daily 9–7:30; Sep–May, daily 9–5. Closed 1 Jan, 25 Dec, Greek Orthodox Easter Sun
- Inexpensive
- Café on site (£)
- From Limassol

Kolossi Castle

Kourion

INFORMATION

✚ C4

✉ Off the Limassol to Pafos road

☎ 2599 1048

🕐 Jul–Aug, daily 8–7:30; Sep–May, daily 8–5. Excavations are still in progress and some parts of the site may be closed at times.

💷 Inexpensive

🍴 Café in the tourist pavilion (£)

🚌 From Limassol

↔ Kolossi (► 29), Temple of Apollo Hylates (► 53)

❓ Classical dramas or productions of Shakespeare are performed in summer.

Kourion is the most important archaeological site in the Greek part of the island, impressively perched on the cliffs overlooking the sea.

There has been some sort of settlement here since 3300 BC, the very early Neolithic period, but the first significant town was probably built by the Mycenaeans around 1400 BC. It reached the height of its powers under the Romans and it is that influence which is the most evident from the ruins. Thereafter it went into decline as it suffered from the attentions of Arab raiders and the population moved inland. Excavations started in 1873 and have continued ever since.

The Theatre presents the most striking image of the whole site. It seated an audience of 3,500 and was probably built by the early Greeks and then extended by the Romans to allow for gladiatorial combat. It is entirely restored and, in summer, performances of plays and concerts are staged.

The Annexe of Eustolios lies just uphill and has an impressive mosaic floor. Further up the hill are the Baths which follow the traditional Roman pattern, with the Frigidarium (cold room), followed by the Tepidarium (warm room) and the Caldarium (hot baths). Various mechanisms for heating the water, along with furnaces and water tanks, are still in evidence.

At the top of the hill, west of the Theatre, is the Building of the Achilles Mosaic. The house dates from about AD 4 and was probably a reception area for visitors. A similar house lies a short distance down the track, where the mosaic shows two gladiators in combat. Also visible are the remains of an aqueduct which brought water to the Fountain House. Opposite the Fountain House is the 5th-century Basilica.

Ancient Greek pillars at Kourion

Kykkos Monastery

The Kykkos monastery is the largest and richest foundation in Cyprus and is known throughout the Orthodox world.

Kykkos is sited high and alone in the hills of western Cyprus, but even at 1,318m above sea level it is overlooked by higher ground. In summer its cloisters and courtyards are cool; in winter when the mist descends, the temperature drops alarmingly. Cypriots make pilgrimages to Kykkos from all over southern Cyprus, and hundreds may visit in a weekend. Kykkos was built about 900 years ago for its icon, the painting of which is attributed to St Luke. The present construction with two main courtyards is not of great antiquity – fires destroyed earlier buildings and nothing is older than the 19th century. In contrast with the spartan conditions of earlier times, today's monks have many modern comforts. Even so, over the years the community has dwindled from hundreds to a handful.

The famous icon is called *Elousa*. It has been encased in silver for 200 years and anyone attempting to gaze directly on it does so under sufferance of horrible punishment. Photography is not permitted. There is also a small one-room museum with items of interest from the monastery's past, mainly religious regalia and books. In 1926, a novice called Michael Mouskos came to the monastery. He was to become Archbishop Makarios III, and President of Cyprus. During the later EOKA campaign the monastery was used by the guerillas for communications and handling supplies. Makarios is buried on the hill called Throni, directly above the monastery.

INFORMATION

➕ B3
✉ West of Pedoulas, western Troodos
☎ Museum: 2294 2736
🕐 Monastery: daily
   Museum: Mar–Oct daily 10–6; Nov–Apr daily 10–4
🎟 Free; museum inexpensive
🍴 Café nearby (£)

A solemn-faced depiction of the Madonna and Child at Kykkos

Kyrenia (Girne)

INFORMATION

⊞ C2

🍴 Cafés around the
harbour (£–££)

Kyrenia is unmatched in the rest of Cyprus. This eulogy attributes nothing to the town. It is all to do with the harbour and its magnificent setting.

Certainly the old buildings of the quayside, with the exception of the customs houses, have all been reconstituted as restaurants and bars; nevertheless, everything seems just perfect, day or night.

A huge cylindrical bastion from Venetian times forms the east end of the harbour, a minaret rises up in the middle ground and an Anglican spire in the west. Mountain ridges and summits run unbroken into the hazy distance.

The harbour is Kyrenia's principal attraction

Kyrenia Castle

The origins of the castle are Lusignan, but it was the Venetians who made it impregnable. Inside, sunlight streams through hidden windows.

Entry into the complex structure is over the moat, now dry, to reach a gatehouse. Progress is then up a ramp, passing a small Byzantine chapel and then on to the northwest tower. Here is the tomb of Sadik Paşa, killed in 1570, during the Turkish conquest of Cyprus.

Various routes can be taken to complete a tour of the castle, care being needed to keep clear of the unguarded battlements and drops. There is much of interest, but the shipwreck museum should not be missed. It houses the oldest ship ever raised from the seabed. The blackened hulk, astonishingly well preserved, is no less than 2,300 years old. It was lifted from the sea in 1968–69.

INFORMATION

➕ C2
✉ Harbourside
🕐 Jun–Sep, daily 9–7;
    Oct–May, daily 9–1,
    2–4:45
💰 Expensive

The 2,300-year-old wreck in the Kyrenia Castle museum

Lala Mustafa Paşa Mosque

The building has been a mosque for over 400 years but the architecture is distinctively that of a Latin cathedral.

There is a single minaret, well executed but certainly out of place. Even so, it is still possible to admire the splendid six-light window of the west front. Three portals lead to the impressive interior, where Moslem simplicity has enabled the fine Gothic nave to survive the loss of its Christian decoration.

Lala Mustafa was the victorious commander of the Ottoman Turks when they broke into Famagusta in 1571. Surprisingly, the mosque only received his name in 1954, before which it was called the Mosque of Santa Sophia.

Gothic nave of Lala Mustafa Paşa Mosque

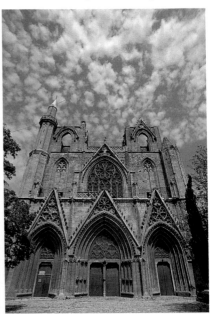

Lara

A remote and beautiful area where the land sweeps up to the high hills and turtles come ashore to breed.

Lara is the name of a headland with sandy bays on each side. This splendid coast continues on up to Koppos Island, opposite which the rough road gives out, and then on to the distant north cape.

The nearest outpost is Agios Georgios, hardly a village but having a church and harbour and, of course, restaurants. It sees the last of the hard surface road, and from now on the track is terrible, best attempted with a jeep-type vehicle. And there is quite a lot of it – 8km in all, with one steep area that is a real test of nerve on the cliff edge. Thicket, thorn and mimosa border the road, and only by chance or local knowledge can sandy coves on the rocky shore be found. The beaches of Lara itself are easier to discover, with a sweeping bay to the north and a smaller one to the south.

Lara is now a popular destination for there are regular boat trips from Pafos calling at Agios Georgios on the way. Such splendid beaches and scenery would attract visitors in any circumstances, but there is further incentive – Lara's famous turtles. In an attempt to secure the future of these beleaguered and precious amphibians a hatchery has been established at Lara. Paradoxically, this was accompanied by great publicity and many make the trip in the hope of seeing them; in fact there is no certainty of this – much depends on the cycle of the breeding season. In 2002 the future of this beautiful and ecologically important coastline was secured when the government declared it an area in which no building development is allowed.

INFORMATION

➕ A3
✉ Western Cyprus, north of Pafos
🏛 Free
🍴 Café near the headland (£)

Newly-hatched turtles

Larnaka

Larnaka is a significant tourist and commercial centre and is a very convenient base for exploring the island, although its own sites of interest are a little limited.

The modern city is built on the remains of ancient Kition which was, according to the legend, established by one of Noah's grandsons in the 13th century BC. Out of this settlement Larnaka became an important trading centre, from where the island's main export of copper was shipped, and it has long had a large foreign population.

The town can be very busy at rush hour and the narrow streets and one way system do not help the foreign driver. Visitors should try to park quickly and explore on foot. The pedestrianised seafront is lined with cafés and at the far end of the promenade is a large marina with berths for 450 yachts. Larnaka is the main yachting centre of the island and the port facilities here attract boats from all over the eastern Mediterranean. There is a very popular beach in the

Turkish Fort and Medieval Museum

centre of town, but it is man-made and certainly not among the best on the island. The seafront road provides amenities for the captive tourist market with an abundance of cafés, restaurants and ice-cream sellers.

Larnaka has a long history, but much of the evidence of that history has been covered by the sprawl of the modern city. However, the enthusiast will be able to track down archaeological remains and historic churches.

Lefkara

The village is divided into two halves, Pano (upper) and Kato (lower) Lefkara and is a popular tourist destination. Visitors who prefer to avoid the crowds should come in the early morning.

Lefkara is known for its lace, called *lefkaritika* and first became famous in 1481 when Leonardo da Vinci ordered some for Milan Cathedral. It then became popular with local Venetian ladies and the lacemaking industry took off. The tradition continues to flourish today and rather ferocious ladies will offer their wares vigorously to passing tourists. Those wishing to buy should take care to ensure that it is the genuine article and not imported. There are also a number of silver-ware shops.

The main street of Pano Lefkara is now designed to cater for tourists but the narrow alleys to either side are still peaceful places to wander. There is also a small museum of lacemaking and silverware, signposted from the main street.

The lower half of the village is often neglected but is worth a visit. Its church of Archangel Michael has some beautiful 18th-century icons and there are very good views across the hills from outside the building. The houses in this part of the village are painted in a distinctive blue and white and its streets are extremely narrow and therefore traffic free.

INFORMATION

⊞ C3

✉ 9km northwest of junction 13 of the Nicosia–Limassol motorway

◉ Museum: Mon–Thu 9:30–4, Fri–Sat 10–4

▥ Inexpensive

☎ 2434 2326

🍽 Cafés in the main street of the upper village (£)

Lefkara is famous for silverware and lace

Limassol

INFORMATION

➕ C4
ℹ️ Spyrou Araouzou 115A
☎ 2536 2756
🍴 Many (£–££)

Limassol's main claim to fame is that King Richard the Lionheart was shipwrecked here and married his fiancée Berengaria in the town.

Wall detail at Limassol

The Knights Hospitallers developed Limassol as a trading post based on export of the Commandaria wine which they made in the vineyards surrounding Kolossi. However, it was only in the 19th century that its major asset, the deep water port, began to be appreciated and the town grew into a significant commercial centre.

In recent years Limassol has seen massive tourist development along the wide and noisy approach road on a stretch of coast without good beaches. It is a modern town but it does not lack atmosphere and offers good shopping, nightlife and restaurants. The carnival in spring and the wine festival in early September are particularly lively times to visit the town.

The sites of Limassol are easily explored on foot (▶ 15), indeed those coming by car should be prepared for traffic problems and a fiendishly complicated one-way system. The main historical site is the castle and medieval museum. There are also a couple of mosques, with distinctive minarets, serving as reminders of a time when Limassol had a Turkish quarter. The main shopping area is around Agiou Andreou Street.

Sunbathing on a breakwater at Limassol

Mevlevi Tekke (Ethnographical Museum)

Nicosia's impressive ethnographical museum was originally the home of the legendary Whirling Dervishes, a sect founded in the 13th century.

The rooms throughout the museum have a simple elegance, complete with a splendid minstrels' gallery looking down on where the Dervishes, heads lowered in contemplation, would stretch out their arms and spin at ever increasing speed. In 1925 Kemal Ataturk forbade the dancing in an attempt to modernise Turkish culture. After 20 years the ruling was relaxed and the dance celebrated once more. To one side is an interesting collection of costumes, wedding dresses and musical instruments associated with the history of this famously idiosyncratic sect. Adjoining is a long mausoleum containing 15 tombs, the resting places of important Dervishes.

INFORMATION

* b1
* Girne Caddesi, Nicosia
* Jun–Sep, Mon–Fri 7:30–2; Oct–May, Mon–Fri 9–1, 2–4:45
* Inexpensive

Left: medieval inscriptions in the museum
Below: Dervishes whirling

Nicosia's Cyprus Museum

On the Greek side of Nicosia, the Cyprus Museum displays a vast range of artefacts demonstrating the city's wealth of historical importance.

The museum houses most of the important finds from sites across Cyprus – neolithic artefacts, Bronze-Age vases and clay figurines, Mycenaean objects from Kourion and some surprisingly sophisticated pottery.

Two thousand figurines found at Agia Irini are displayed as they were found, gathered around a single altar. A wide range of sculptures are on show, as well as a huge bronze statue of Emperor Septimius and the famous green-horned god from Enkomi. There are impressive artefacts from Salamis, the first City of Cyprus, as well as some mosaics and a reconstruction of a rock cut tomb.

The Cyprus Museum protects many of the islands finest artefacts

Nicosia's Walled City

Eleven stout bastions superimposed on a circular plan give the city its distinctive and unique form. Much has survived the centuries.

INFORMATION

- a2/c1
- Centre of Nicosia
- Cafés at Laïki Geitonia, Famagusta Gate, Attatürk Square (£)

Nicosia's formidable ramparts, so masterfully constructed by the Venetians, remain substantially intact, although Pafos Gate to the west is battered and Girne (Kyrenia) Gate's situation ruined. Famagusta Gate has fared better, although it is now a cultural centre, perhaps something of a comedown for what was the important eastern entrance into the city. A lesser but similar indignity has been inflicted on the wide moat (always intended to be dry): this deep and formidable barrier to full scale attack is now a collection of very pleasant gardens, car parks and football pitches. In the end the great walls did not save Nicosia; the Turks broke through in 1570 after a siege of 70 days – a bloody event, with the victors celebrating in an orgy of slaughter.

Today Ledra and Onasagoras Streets in the Greek sector are thriving, bustling places, and the small shops of all kinds are continuously busy. A little to the east the reconstructed buildings known as Laïki Geitonia are popular with visitors. In the Turkish part of town development moves at a somewhat slower pace.

Top: bustling Nicosia
Above: Famagusta Gate

Along the backstreets are areas that are conspicuously decrepit. This is not entirely regrettable, as low overheads have enabled a Bohemian quarter to grow up around Famagusta Gate, with bars, cafés, a bookshop or two and a small theatre. Close by, and including Ermou Street, is a renovated neighbourhood. The buildings remain much as before, but wearing new clothes. Small, interesting squares, once rough underfoot, are now smoothly paved.

41

Pafos

INFORMATION

✚ B4

ℹ 3 Gladstanos Street

☎ 2692 32841

The first settlement dates from the 4th century BC and Pafos played an important role in early Cypriot history.

After the 4th century AD it declined and, although its fortunes improved slightly under British administration, it is only in the last 30 years, as transport links improved, that Pafos has seen real growth. Tourist development, in particular, took off after the construction of the new international airport in 1983. The old town on top of the hill changes little. However, on the coastal strip the tourist development is extensive. Still, the harbour and its immediate environs remain attractive. The richness of its archaeological heritage places ancient Nea Pafos on UNESCO's list of World Heritage Sites.

The modern town is split into two; upper and lower Pafos, also known as Kitma and Kato Pafos. The upper town is where you will find the main commercial centre, shops and modern museums.

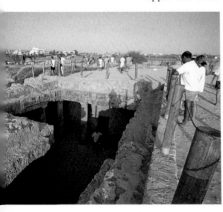

Tombs of the Kings in Kato Pafos

The lower town contains most of the archaeological remains which are spread out across the area. Some are in formal sites, but do not be surprised to come across ancient ruins among modern houses. The harbour is the focus of the lower town and is a pleasant place to stroll in its own right. It is also the haunt of Pafos' most famous resident; the pelican. Cafés are strung out along the seafront and there are plenty of places to stop and eat or have a drink and watch the yachts although it can be busy at the height of summer.

Pafos Mosaics

Impressive, well-preserved Roman mosaics depict colourful scenes from Greek mythology.

The mosaics were found in five large 3rd-century villas which probably belonged to wealthy Roman noblemen. The House of Dionysos was the first to be excavated, after a passing shepherd turned up some fragments of mosaics. The depictions include that of Ganymede being taken to Olympus by an eagle. The most famous mosaic is that of the triumph of Dionysos as he heads across the skies in a chariot drawn by leopards.

The House of Aion displays a very fine series of mosaics which were discovered in 1983. The five scenes starting from the top left show Leda and the Swan; the baby Dionysos; then the middle panel depicts a beauty contest being judged by Aion; on the bottom row is the triumphant procession of Dionysos and the punishment of a musician, Marsyas, who had challenged Apollo to a musical contest and lost. These mosaics date from the late 4th century.

The House of Orpheus contains representations of Amazon, Hercules and the Lion of Nemea, alongside a very impressive mosaic featuring Orpheus surrounded by animals who are listening to his music.

The main mosaic in the House of Theseus is that of Theseus killing the minotaur, although there are some others featuring Achilles and Neptune. The mosaics here are less well preserved than in other areas of the site. A new area – the House of the Four Seasons – was unearthed in 1992. Mosaics showing the Gods of the Seasons and a variety of hunting scenes were found. As excavations continue, some parts may not be open to the public.

INFORMATION

🞦 B4

✉ Within the World Heritage Site, a short distance inland from the harbour

☎ 2630 6217

🕐 Jun–Aug, daily 8–7:30; Sep–May, daily 9–5. Closed 1 Jan, 25 Dec, Greek Orthodox Easter Sun

🎟 Moderate (includes Odeion ➤ 53 and Saranda Kolones ➤ 54)

🍴 Cafés at the harbour (££)

↔ St Paul's Pillar (➤ 59), Pafos Fort (➤ 54)

The mosaics at Pafos are among the finest in the world

Petra tou Romiou

INFORMATION

➕ B4
✉ 24km east of Pafos
🍽 Two cafés, one in the tourist pavilion (£)

Petra tou Romiou – the Rock of Romios – provides a spectacular scene against the backdrop of white cliffs.

This is one of the most photographed sites on the whole island. There are two official places to stop – one close to the rock, just back from the shore, where there is a café and a car park, the other higher up in the cliffs, where there is a tourist pavilion. However, the best view, coming from Limassol, is on the final bend before the road starts to descend; some scrubland on the left makes a convenient layby.

Legend states that this was the birthplace of Aphrodite, where she emerged from the foaming water. The beach itself is rather shingly, and it is not ideal for swimming because it gets rough around the rocks, but it is worth stopping to soak up the mysterious atmosphere.

Sunset silhouettes
Petra tou Romiou

Salamis

The legendary founder of Salamis, an impressive archaeological site, was the Greek hero Teucer, brother of Ajax and son of Telamon.

In the 7th century BC Salamis was the first City of Cyprus. It was not until the Roman occupation, centuries later, that it was succeeded by Pafos in the west. In AD 350 the Byzantines changed the city's name to Constantia, and restored its status as the capital. There was much subsequent rebuilding due to earthquakes, but in the 7th century attacks by Arabs left the city in ruins.

In high summer a visit is a memorable occasion, although only the most determined will be able to stay the full course in the great heat. However, the Roman Theatre should not be missed, with its restored tiers of seats rising to an impressive height. A little further north are the vents and hypocausts of the Baths, opening on to the Gymnasium, all built by the Romans. This structure, its rows of marble columns plainly evident, was damaged by earthquakes and remodelled in Byzantine times, only to collapse later. The columns that we see today were erected as recently as the 1950s.

South of the Theatre the huge columns of the Granite Forum lie across the site. This northern section of the site was a cultural centre. The Agora is found in the central part, near the Voutra, a 7th-century cistern. Close by are the unimpressive ruins of the Temple of Zeus. 500m northeast, towards the sea, is the Kampanopetra, a large early Christian Basilica which has been only partially excavated. The Ancient Harbour is about 300m southeast, on the shoreline. Across the main road on the western site are the Royal Necropolis and several important tombs.

INFORMATION

- D2
- 10km north of Famagusta
- Jun–Sep, daily 9–7; Oct–May, daily 9–1, 2–4:45
- Moderate
- Café near north entrance (£)

Statue at Salamis

Selimiye Mosque

INFORMATION

➕ c2
✉ Selimiye Sokagi, Nicosia
🕐 Daily
🖐 Free

This impressive building was a Christian masterpiece before becoming a mosque of the Ottoman Turks, the most important in Cyprus.

The elevations of magnificent windows, portals and buttresses are worryingly discordant; the reason – the soaring minarets. They are notable landmarks in the walled city, and their imposition on the west front by the Turks reflects the momentous events of 1570–71 when the Turks subjugated the city.

The original cathedral was started in 1209 and substantially completed 117 years later. In reality it was never quite finished, work carrying on long after the consecration.

Everything changed with the arrival of the Turks. All the Christian decoration of the cathedral was destroyed. Soon after, work was started on the minarets and the building became the cathedral of Santa Sophia until the name was changed to the Selimiye Mosque in 1954.

In the cathedral-like Selimiye Mosque in Nicosia

St Hilarion Castle

This fortified monastery, besieged then taken by Richard the Lionheart in 1191, has spectacular views over Kyrenia and the northern coast.

Richard the Lionheart laid siege to the castle in 1191, and after four days emperor Isaac Comnenos surrendered. Today the Turkish military controls the heights around the castle, and it is a significant place to advertise their presence.

This is no compact, easily visited site. There are lower, middle and upper wards, with quite a distance between each and a steep climb to the upper section. The big compensation for the effort – reasonably substantial in the summer heat – is the unbelievable view. The north shore is directly below and Turkey is plainly visible in the clear air of the cooler months. East and west a spectacular line of peaks and ridges run into the distance.

St Hilarion, it seems, was a recluse who found refuge on these heights, and built a retreat here. A monastery was established on the site in the 11th century, and was later fortified and then extended by the Lusignans. The lower ward housed the garrison and their horses. A tunnel leads on to the middle ward and a small Byzantine church. Some steps descend to a hall, which may have been a refectory, or banqueting chamber. Adjacent is a belvedere and café. The view over the coast is exceptional.

The path to the upper ward climbs steadily to the mountain top. Even then not everything is accessible, although St John's tower, in its precipitous location, can be reached by a short detour. The Queen's window is perhaps the place to stop and rest.

INFORMATION

- ➕ C2
- ✉ High in the hills west of Kyrenia
- 🕐 Jun–Sep, daily 9–5; Oct–May, daily 9–1, 2–4:45
- ✋ Moderate
- 🍴 Café at the gate (£)
- ↔ Bellapais Abbey (➤ 25)

The view from St Hilarion

Troodos Mountains

INFORMATION

🟦 C3
✉ Central Cyprus
🍴 Cafés at Troodos village, Platres, Foini, Kakopetria and other villages (£–££)

Despite their elevation, these are friendly, rounded hills with a multitude of charming villages hidden in the pine-covered folds.

The Troodos is an extensive area, running from west of Larnaka to the high ground of Mount Olympus, then falling gradually to the western coast. Terraced vineyards shape the lower southern slopes, with Aleppo pine covering the higher ground. Summits may be tree-covered or adorned with spiky scrub, relieved occasionally with dried flowers. Northern slopes are different again, dark poplars stand out in the valleys alongside golden oak and rock rose. Summer days are cooler on the high ground and a big attraction in winter is the snow, with skiing on Mount Olympus.

Goats take to the road in the Troodos Mountains

The most impressive of Cyprus' celebrated monasteries are in the Troodos. Chrysorrogiatissa, standing in splendid terrain, is about 45km from Pafos. Kykkos (▶ 31) is more convenient for Limassol, but still a half-day's excursion. In the east is Machairas, less splendid but well worth a visit.

Regrettably few seek out the small Byzantine churches of Panagia tou Araka and Stavros tou Agiasmati near Lagoudera on the north side of the range. This is understandable, because it is a long drive, but their frescoes are extraordinary.

In western Cyprus the forest takes over, and Cedar Valley (▶ 20) is renowned for its giant timbers. Fortunately for the peace of this marvellous area few people seem prepared to negotiate the difficult roads.

CYPRUS'
best

Museums

CAMELS PACKED AWAY

In the 15th century the Venetians built a series of bridges over the rivers that cut into the Troodos Mountains. They were for pack animals, particularly camels, to carry copper ore from Mylikouri, Kaminaria, and Foini, high in the hills, to Pafos for export. Alas the camel has gone the way of the export trade. The last census in 1965 counted only 90. Today there is perhaps one, or possibly two, giving rides to holidaymakers in Pafos.

Jug from 7th century BC

ARCHBISHOP MAKARIOS CULTURAL CENTRE (BYZANTINE MUSEUM), NICOSIA

The main exhibits in the museum are the 6th-century Kanakaria Mosaics. Also on show are a large number of icons from churches around the island.
➕ c2 ✉ Archbishopric, Nicosia ☎ 2243 0008 🕐 Mon–Fri 9–4:30, Sat 9–1 🖐 Moderate 🍴 Cafés nearby (£)

HADJIGEORGAKIS KORNESIOS HOUSE, (ETHNOGRAPHICAL MUSEUM), NICOSIA

In a house once belonging to the Great Dragoman of Cyprus, Hadjigeorgakis, at the end of the 18th century, this museum contains a range of fine artefacts.
➕ c2 ✉ Patriarchou Grigoriou Street, Nicosia ☎ 2230 5316 🕐 Mon–Fri 9–5:30 🖐 Inexpensive 🍴 Cafés nearby (£)

LEVENTIS MUSEUM, NICOSIA

Well set out and modest in size, covering the whole period from prehistoric times to the British colonial period and modern times.
➕ b2 ✉ Ippokratous Street, Nicosia ☎ 2266 1475 🕐 Tue–Sun 10–4:30. Closed 1 Jan, 25 Dec, Greek Orthodox Easter Sun 🖐 Free

PAFOS DISTRICT ARCHAEOLOGICAL MUSEUM

This museum houses finds from local excavations (Pegeia, Polis, Lemba). Most fascinating is room 3, with marble Roman eyeballs and clay hot water bottles in the shape of the part of the body they were to warm.
➕ B4 ✉ Dighenis Street, Pafos ☎ 2630 6215 🕐 Mon–Fri 9–5, Sat–Sun 10–1. Closed 1 Jan, 25 Dec, Greek Orthodox Easter Sun 🖐 Inexpensive 🍴 Cafés opposite (£)

PAFOS ETHNOGRAPHICAL MUSEUM

The private collection of George Eliades, a local professor, ranging from neolithic to modern times.
➕ B4 ✉ 1 Exo Vrisis Street ☎ 2693 2010 🕐 Mar–Nov Mon–Sat 9:30–5:30, Sun 10–1; Dec–Feb Mon–Sat 9:30–5, Sun 10–1 🖐 Inexpensive 🍴 Cafés nearby (£)

PIERIDES MUSEUM, LARNAKA

The private collection of antiquities of Demetrius Pierides, covering the neolithic to the Middle Ages and including artefacts from ancient Marion near Polis. Some 3,600 exhibits are displayed in the Pierides family's fine 19th-century house.
➕ D3 ✉ Zinonos Kitieos Street, Larnaka ☎ 2481 4555 🕐 Mon–Thu 9–4, Fril, Sat 9–1. Closed 1 Jan, 25 Dec, Greek Orthodox Easter Sun 🖐 Moderate 🍴 Cafés nearby (£)

Monasteries

In the Top 25

8 Kykkos Monastery (► 31)

AGÍA NAPA MONASTERY

Built in the 16th century over a cave in which an icon of the Virgin Mary was supposedly found. Within a century the monastery had grown rich, owning much land. It was abandoned in the 18th century but later restored under British rule.

🗵 E3 ✉ Centre of Agía Napa village 🕐 Daily 💷 Free
🍴 Many cafés nearby (££)

AGIOS LAZAROS CHURCH

Legend states that Lazaros, raised from the dead by Christ, was buried here; but his remains were stolen and his tomb in the south apse is empty. The church was built in the 9th century and restored in the 17th.

🗵 D3 ✉ Agiou Lazarou Street, Larnaka ☎ Museum: 2465 2498
🕐 Apr–Aug, Mon–Sun 8–12:30, 3:30–6:30; Sep–Mar, Mon–Sun
8–12:30, 2:30–5. Museum: closed Sun 💷 Museum: inexpensive

AGIOS NEOFYTOS MONASTERY

Saint Neofytos lived in caves cut from the hillside in 1159. He added three chambers, decorated with religious wall paintings. Those in the sanctuary are the best preserved.

🗵 B3 ✉ 9km north of Pafos 🕐 Apr–Sep, daily 9–1, 2–6;
Oct–Mar, daily 9–4 💷 Inexpensive 🍴 Café outside (£)

ASINOU CHURCH (PANAGIA FORVIOTISSA)

Asinou has remained unscathed for 900 years and its frescoes make it the best of Cyprus' painted churches.

🗵 C3 ✉ Near Nikitari, Troodos Mountains 🕐 Ask in Nikitari for
the priest with the key 💷 Free

PANAGIA ANGELOKTISTOS CHURCH (KITI CHURCH)

Panagia Angeloktistos, which means 'built by angels', was constructed in the 11th century on the remains of an earlier 5th-century church. It has many ornate icons but its main attraction is its mosaic.

🗵 D3 ✉ Edge of the village on road to Mazotos ☎ 2442 4646
🕐 Daily 8–12, 2–4. If locked ask for the key at the nearby café
💷 Donation 🍴 Café nearby (£) 🚌 From Larnaka

STAVROVOUNI MONASTERY

At 690m the monastery commands spectacular views. There has been a religious community here since AD 327 when St Helena brought a fragment of the True Cross from Jerusalem. It is claimed that the piece is still there. The monks do not allow women inside.

🗵 D3 ✉ 40km west of Larnaka 🕐 Apr–Aug, daily 8–12, 3–6;
Sep–Mar, daily 8–12, 2–5 💷 Free (men only)

ST PAUL AND ST BARNABAS

St Barnabas brought Christianity to Cyprus. Accompanied by St Paul, he landed at Salamis then travelled to Pafos. The story of their travels is told in Acts in the Bible, which relates how St Paul blinded a local sorcerer and so impressed the Roman consul of Pafos that he became a convert to Christianity.

Painted interior of Asinou church

51

Ancient Sites

OLD THREAT REMAINS

The ancient city of Pafos was destroyed twice by earthquakes. It has remained susceptible to tremors and in October 1996 a tremor measuring 6.1 on the Richter Scale was felt, causing landslides and some structural damage.

AMATHOUS

The archaeological remains of Amathous are spread over a wide area and include a rock-cut tomb in the grounds of the Amathus Beach Hotel. The most easily accessible ruins are of the Agora, in a fenced site just off the main road on the inland side. This was the market area and although it is a relatively small site there are a large number of pillars still visible which make it quite impressive. Up a track from the Agora is the Acropolis and the remains of a Temple to Aphrodite. Some of the site is now underwater, offering exciting opportunities for divers and snorkellers.

➕ C4 ✉ 8km east of Limassol ⏰ Jul–Aug, daily 9–7:30; Sep–Jun, daily 9–5 🚌 From Limassol and Larnaka 💷 Inexpensive

The Temple of Apollo Hylates near Pafos

KHIROKITIA (CHOIROKOITIA)

The oldest archaeological site on the island dates from 6800 BC when it was home to as many as 2,000 people who farmed the surrounding land.

The most distinctive feature of the settlement is the beehive-shape houses, built close together and linked by narrow passageways. The inhabitants tended to bury their dead under the floor of the house and then build on top; some houses have revealed up to eight different periods of habitation.

➕ C3 ✉ Off Junction 14, Nicosia–Limassol motorway ☎ 2432 2710 ⏰ Jun–Aug, Mon–Fri 9–7:30, Sat, Sun 9–5; Sep–May, daily 9–5. Closed 1 Jan, 25 Dec, Greek Orthodox Easter Sun 💷 Inexpensive

KITION

Remains of the ancient city are found at a number of sites across Larnaka. The most visible ruins are on Leontiou Machaira near the Archaeological Museum. The trenches and walls date from the 12th and 13th centuries BC, when they enclosed the city. You can make out the traces of a Phoenician temple and the sharp eyed may detect the images of ships carved into the south wall.

➕ D3 ✉ Leontiou Machaira Street, Larnaka ⏰ Mon–Wed, Fri 9–2:30, Thu 9–2:30, 3–5. Closed 1 Jan, PM Jul–Aug, 25 Dec 💷 Inexpensive

PAFOS ODEION

This theatre has been partially restored to give an interesting impression of how it would have been. It was built in the 2nd century AD, during the Roman period, then suffered earthquake damage in the 7th century and was abandoned.

➕ B4 ✉ Within the World Heritage Site, inland from the harbour 🕐 Jun–Aug daily 8–7:30; Sep–-May daily 8–5 ⬤ Moderate includes mosaics and Saranda Kolones

SOLI

Soli's founders came from Greece and created a city destined to play a major role in the struggle against Persian rule in the 5th and 4th centuries BC. However only later Roman works survive. They cut a theatre out of a rocky hillside overlooking Morfou Bay. Today most of this substantial work is a reconstruction.

➕ B2 ✉ Near Gemikonagi 🕐 Jun–Sep, daily 9–7; Oct–May, daily 9–1, 2–4:45 ⬤ Moderate

TEMPLE OF APOLLO HYLATES

The temple was first used as a place of pilgrimage in the 8th century BC although the ruins seen today are from AD 100, when it was rebuilt after an earthquake. The circular remains of the votive pit have yielded a wealth of ancient artefacts.

➕ B4 ✉ Limassol–Pafos Road ☎ 2599 1049 🕐 Jul–Aug, daily 9–7:30; Sep–Jun, daily 9–5. Closed 1 Jan, 25 Dec, Greek Orthodox Easter Sun ⬤ Inexpensive

TOMBS OF THE KINGS

The 100 tombs on the site cover a wide area and date from about the 3rd century BC. Steps lead down inside the tombs, often into a whole series of passageways. The chambers near the centre of the site get busy and it is worth walking a little further away to those on the edge of the area, which are just as impressive.

➕ B4 ✉ 2km northwest of Pafos centre ☎ 2630 6295 🕐 Jun–Aug, daily 8:30–7:30; Sep–May, daily 8–5 ⬤ Inexpensive 🍽 Café on site (£) 🚌 10, 15 from Pafos

VOUNI PALACE

The road to ruined Vouni Palace spirals spectacularly upwards, a splendid area where the Troodos Mountains meet the northern shore. The palace once had apartments, baths and courtyards. Little is known but it was built in the 5th century BC by a pro-Persian king from Marion, possibly to counter the power of nearby Soli, a city loyal to the Greeks. The bathing rooms are comparable to those of the Romans, but they are centuries earlier. At the top of the hill are the ruins of the Greek-style Temple of Athena.

➕ B2 ✉ Near Gemikonagi 🕐 Jun–Sep, daily 10–5; Oct–May, daily 9–1, 2–2:45 ⬤ Moderate

ON THE LINE

The Ledra Palace Hotel used to be the main luxury hotel in Nicosia. Now standing on the Green Line, it is home to British United Nations troops and is still marked with bullet holes from the 1974 conflict. It is used for meetings between the two sides, both official and unofficial.

In the Tombs of the Kings

53

Castles

BRITISH MILITARY BASES

Some 256sq km of Cyprus is British territory, contained within the three main military bases at Dhekalia, Akrotiri and Episkopi. These areas are subject to British law and are officially known as Sovereign Base Areas.

KANTARA CASTLE

Kantara is the most easterly of the great Lusignan fortresses of the northern shore. At 600m above sea level its ramparts crown rocky crags, with the north shore way below and stretching into the distance. Most of the castle is a ruin, although the formidable outer wall is substantially intact. Entrance is through a ruined barbican and two towers. Steps lead on to vaulted chambers and medieval toilets.

➕ E2 ✉ Near Kantara village 🕐 Jun–Sep, daily 10–5; Oct–May, daily 9–1, 2–4:45 💷 Inexpensive 🍴 Cafés in Kantara village (£)

LIMASSOL CASTLE

The main buildings of the castle were constructed in the 14th century on the site of an earlier Byzantine

structure. The chapel in which Richard the Lionheart and Berengaria were married is no longer standing. The castle was used by the Turks as a prison and later as British army headquarters.

➕ C4 ✉ Eirinis Street, near the old port, Limassol ☎ 2530 5419 🕐 Mon–Sat 9–5, Sun 10–1. Closed 1 Jan, 25 Dec 💷 Inexpensive 🍴 Many cafés nearby (£)

PAFOS FORT

Originally the harbour was guarded by two castles built by the Lusignans in the 13th century. Both were badly damaged when the Turks attacked in 1570, but one was restored and used by the Turks as a prison. Public access is across a drawbridge.

➕ B4 ✉ Harbour Wall, Pafos 🕐 Jun–Aug, daily 9–7:30; Sep–May, daily 9–5. Closed 1 Jan, 25 Dec, Greek Orthodox Easter Sun 💷 Inexpensive

SARANDA KOLONES (FORTY COLUMNS) BYZANTINE FORT, PAFOS

This fortress dates from around the 7th century, though it was rebuilt in the 12th century. It was probably established to protect the city from seaborne raiders until it was replaced by the forts on the breakwater. The remains of many of the original columns, the central keep and some of the towers on the thick outer walls can be made out.

Saranda Kolones Fort in Pafos

➕ B4 ✉ Within the World Heritage Site, inland from the harbour 🕐 Jun–Aug daily 8–7:30; Sep–Mar daily 8–5 💷 Moderate inlcudinges mosaics and Odeion 🍴 Cafés nearby (££)

Beaches

AKROTIRI PENINSULA

The area contains a good beach, a salt lake and a historic church. Lady's Mile beach is sandy and offers safe swimming in very shallow sea. The far end is closed off by the British Base at Akrotiri.

🔲 C4 ✉ Southwest of Limassol ⊚ Agios Nikolaos ton Gaton: daily. Closed during siesta 🍴 Cafés on beach (£) 🖳 Free

AVDIMOU BEACH

Avdimou beach is a really good, long, sandy stretch although the water becomes deep very quickly. It is part of the British Sovereign Base. There are small tavernas at each end of the beach.

🔲 B4 ✉ 3km off main road, opposite turning to Avdimou village 🍴 Taverna on beach (£)

CORAL BAY

This is a popular resort, with shops, hotels and restaurants. The sea is a beautiful turquoise but the shoreline is losing to developers.

🔲 A3 ✉ 13km north of Pafos 🚌 10, 15 from Pafos old town 🍴 Cafés on the clifftops (££)

GOVERNOR'S BEACH

The beach is reached down some steps cut out of the tall white cliffs. The astonishingly dark sand is its most distinctive feature.

🔲 C4 ✉ Junction 16 Nicosia to Limassol motorway 🍴 Cafés on clifftop (£)

NISSI BEACH

Nissi Beach is where tourist development in this area started. A pleasant sandy beach, which can be very crowded in summer, with a rocky island just offshore accessible by a sand bar.

🔲 E3 ✉ 2km west of Agia Napa 🍴 Several cafés (£)

POMOS

There are some wonderful quiet beaches along this section of coast. Just beyond Pomos Point is a small fishing harbour and sheltered beach. At Kato Pyrgos, further east, there is another isolated beach. No further progress is possible owing to the Turkish military.

🔲 B2 ✉ 22km northwest of Polis 🍴 Cafés at Kato Pyrgos (£) 🚌 Limited service from Polis to Pomos, at 11, 2, 4, 6; Sat 11, 2:30, 4

LOCALS AND SWIMMING

For a long time the local population seemed somewhat baffled by the visiting tourists' passion for the beach. They are coming to terms with the phenomenon although, even now, for most of the year, Cypriots feel that the sea is far too cold to comtemplate swimming.

Nissi beach

Children's Activities

THE LURE OF WATER

The marinas and waterparks that have sprung up recently in Cyprus almost suggest that previously there was a lack of entertainment for children. Doubtless these expensive ventures will eventually pay off, but the sandy beaches, turquoise seas and swimming pools will always be the better attraction for children. On a cautionary note, as the sun shines fiercely throughout the summer, great care should be taken to avoid a holiday ruined by sunburn.

APHRODITE WATERPARK

Pools, splashes, spiral descents and more.
✉ Geroskipou. off Poseidonos Avenue, Kato Pafos ☎ 9552 7211
🕐 Apr–Oct daily 9–6

BIRD PARK, PAFOS

Parrots, hornbills, toucans and eagles, and many more species. Gazelles, giant tortoises and other reptiles plus an aquarium. Cinemas and a restaurant.
✉ Pegeia on the raod north out of Coral Bay ☎ 2681 3852
🕐 Apr–Sep daily 9–8; Oct–Mar daily 9–5

BOAT TRIPS, LARNAKA

Hour-long trips in glass-bottom boats show the undersea world of Cyprus. Conventional craft offer half- and one-day excursions around Cape Greko and north in to Famagusta Bay.
✉ Agia Napa Harbour 🕐 Daily May–Oct

BOAT TRIPS, LIMASSOL

Sail by catamaran from Limassol Old Port to Cape Gata. Various permutations of time, distance and price.
✉ Relax Catamaran Cruises ☎ 8000 8007

BOAT TRIPS, PAFOS

Glass-bottom boats explore wrecks and rocky islands off Pafos. Conventional boats go along the west coast.
✉ Pafos Harbour 🕐 Apr–Oct daily

CAMEL PARK

Learn about camels, take a ride, or swim in the pool.
✉ Mazatos, 20km southwest of Larnaka ☎ 2499 1243
🕐 Daily 8–6

DINOSAURS PARK

Extinct and robotic they might be but they move convincingly and all with sound effects.
✉ Municipal Gardens, 28 Octovriou Street, Limassol ☎ 2584 3223
🕐 Daily 10–7

DONKEY SANCTUARY

Unwanted donkeys end up here to be cared for by two expatriates from the UK. A visitors' centre provides information and refreshments.
✉ Vouni, 36km northwest of Limassol ☎ 2594 5488 🕐 Mon–Sat 10–4

KARTING CENTER

For children to adults. Mini track of 220m with a main track of 1,600m. Incorporates a Luna Park (funfair). Large restaurant and café.

✉ Dromolaxia, 5km southwest of Larnaka ☎ 7000 7677 ⏲ Daily 9AM–midnight

LA LUNA PARK AND PARKO PALATSO
An assembly of wheels, rides, coasters, trampolines and other stomach-churning creations: the notorious 'Sling Shot' and next to that, the'Sky Coaster'.
✉ Off Nissi Avenue, adjacent to the Napa Tsokkas Hotel Agia Napa
⏲ May–Oct daily; no fixed hours

OASIS LUNA PARK
Big Wheel, scary inclined ride, dodgems and all the fun of the fair.
✉ 107 Georgiou A. Potamos Germasogias, Limassol ☎ 2531 8389
⏲ Times vary but usually daily

REPTILE HOUSE
Native lizards and more exotic creatures.
✉ Old Harbour, Limassol ☎ 2537 2779 ⏲ Daily 9:30–6

SADKO SUBMARINE
The real thing. Deep underwater excursions including the wreck of the *Zinobia* in Larnaka Bay.
☎ 2481 8865; www.sadkosub.com

SNAKE GEORGE
George tries to improve public understanding of snakes with his reptile park.
✉ 15km north of Pafos on the coastal road road to Agios Georgios, behind BP petrol station ☎ 2693 8160 ⏲ Daily 10–sunset

TIME ELEVATOR
The history of Cyprus up to the present is displayed in the advanced digital theatre.
✉ Vasilissis Street, Limassol (behind the Castle) ☎ 2576 2828
⏲ Daily at 9:15, then every 45 mins

WATERWORLD
Exciting slides plus log rolling, river trips and more. Modest karting track next door (separate entry).
✉ 5km west from Agia Napa, along Agia Thekla Road ☎ 2372 4444; email: waterpaark@cytanet.com.cy ⏲ Apr–Oct daily 10–6

WET 'N' WILD WATERPARK
Chutes and other ingenious designs flush williing participants through a multitude of coloured tubes.
✉ Vasileos Pavlou Street, Nicosia ⏲ Apr–Oct daily 10–6

YELLOW SUBMARINE
The underwater views from the lower deck are terrific. There is a snorkelling stop.
✉ Agia Napa Harbour ☎ 9965 8280 ⏲ Departures 12 and 2:30; free ransfers from protaras

ZET KARTING AND LEISURE CENTER
High standard circuit.
✉ Alaykoi Road, Nicosia ☎ 866 6171; www.zetcarting.com

ADMISSION PRICES

Entry into the Luna parks is free. However, the more innovative and exciting rides/experiences are expensive. Water parks with their impressive features are also expensive. The skycoaster is particularly pricey.

On Kourion beach

Cyprus' Best

Walks

COUNTRYSIDE CARE

You should not leave litter in the countryside, cut flowers or plants, or damage structures. Such actions contravene the Forest Law and offenders face prosecution.

WALKING

Many visitors to Cyprus are enthusiastically turning to walking in the cooler months. The Cypriot, however, remains to be converted to the concept, so until recently there were no ramblers' paths or trails. But there are lots of opportunities for walking in the mountains. Large scale maps will be needed on most occasions. The British Ministry of Defence series is invaluable. Try the Department of Lands and Survey in Nicosia for copies (☎ 2280 5504). In the north walkers will have problems with access as many areas are closed off by the military.

There are four walking trails in the Troodos Region. These have been designed by the Cyprus Tourism Organisation (CTO), which provides helpful leaflets listing the flora, geology and other natural features. The trails are not always that well marked and the leaflets are not very detailed, so walkers will need to keep their wits about them (► 83).

ARTEMIS TRAIL

A high level circuit of 6.5km around Mount Olympus, starting a short distance up the road to the summit.

ATALANTE TRAIL

Starts from Troodos Post Office and is 9km long. After about 3km from the start point the trail reaches a spring of clean drinking water.

KALEDONIA TRAIL

This is also known as 'the trail of nightingales' due to its warbling birds. The start is reached by turning off the Platres Road heading down to the summer presidential residence. The trail runs along the banks of the river to the falls and is 3km long.

The view from Makarios' tomb in the Troodos Mountains

PERSEPHONE TRAIL

Offering beautiful scenery, it starts just south of Troodos Square and is about 6.5km there and back.

AKAMAS TRAILS

In the Akamas there are two trails. Both start from the Baths of Aphrodite and are both about 7.5km long, initially heading west of the Baths before going their separate ways.

Free Attractions

FAMAGUSTA GATE

This was once the major entrance into the old city from the south and east. It is set into the old walls and has been restored to house a cultural centre which is used for exhibitions and other events.
✉ Leoforus Athinon, Famagusta ☎ 2243 0877 🕔 Mon–Fri 10–1, 4–7, (5–8 Jun–Aug) 👢 Free 🍴 Cafés nearby (£)

MUNICIPAL GARDENS AND ZOO, LIMASSOL

The Municipal Gardens offer some welcome greenery in a dusty city. It also contains a small zoo, although the animals are kept in very poor conditions. There is a small open-air theatre where there are productions during the summer. The Gardens are also the site of the annual Limassol Wine Festival, held in September. All the local wine companies set up stalls and offer an evening of free wine tasting accompanied by music and dancing.
✉ 28 Oktovriou Street, Limassol ☎ 2558 8345 🕔 Gardens: daylight hours; Zoo: daily 9–6:30 👢 Gardens: free; Zoo: moderate 🍴 Café in the Gardens (£)

ST PAUL'S PILLAR AND AGIA KYRIAKI

This is a small archaeological site in the back streets of Pafos where a large number of columns and other fragments of buildings have been unearthed. Excavations are still taking place and this may mean that parts of the site will be closed off. The archaeologists are not sure what the actual buildings were in this area, although one theory is that it was a Roman Forum. Most people, however, come here to see St Paul's Pillar which stands at the western end of the site. According to legend, St Paul was tied to this stone and given 39 lashes as a punishment for preaching Christianity.
✉ Stassandrou Street, Pafos 🕔 Daylight hours 👢 Free 🍴 Cafés nearby (£)

PANAGIA TOU ARAKA

The church is generally locked, admission being by courtesy of the priest normally found in the village of Lagoudera. It retains the most complete series of wall paintings of the Byzantine period on the island, which were recently restored courtesy of UNESCO.
✉ Lagoudera 🕔 Sun and courtesy of the priest in Lagoudera 👢 Free 🍴 Café in nearby village (£)

CASHING IN

The story of the birth of Aphrodite has inspired many poets and painters ranging from Shelley, Tennyson and Keats to Botticelli whose painting, *The Birth of Venus*, shows Aphrodite rising from the sea in a huge shell. More contemporary but less poetic references can be found in the hundreds of restaurants and souvenir shops which have taken her name.

Wall painting at Panagia tou Araka

Places to Have Lunch

TREE OF IDLENESS

Lawrence Durrell passed some of his leisure time drinking coffee and telling stories under the Tree of Idleness in Beylerbeyi (Bellapais). He warned against this relaxation if work remained to be done. Two adjoining cafés now lay claim to the tree, to the amusement of the late Sabri Tahir, who helped Durrell to buy his village house. He considers they are arguing over the wrong tree.

ANGELOS
Simple food in a cliff-top setting overlooking the sea. Popular with locals and visitors alike.
✉ Governor's Beach ☎ 2563 2806

BUNCH OF GRAPES INN
The building is splendid and unique. The menu is a blend of traditional Cypriot dishes and British and French cuisine.
✉ Pissouri village ☎ 2522 1275

ESPERIA
Excellent seafood in a wonderful position above the turquoise waters of the harbour.
✉ Harbour, Agia Napa ☎ 2372 1635

MELANDA BEACH RESTAURANT
Specialises in seafood.
✉ Avdimou beach (not jetty) 30km west of Limassol ☎ 2599 1700

MELITZIS RESTAURANT
The best of Cyprus' village food.
✉ 42 Pyale Pasha, Larnaka ☎ 2465 5867

PETRA TOU ROMIOU RESTAURANT AND FISH TAVERN
Fabulous views over the celebrated rock.
✉ Short distance off the main road ☎ 2699 6005

SET FISH RESTAURANT
Good harbour position. Fresh fish every day.
✉ Kyrenia Harbour

VANGELIS
Popular with locals; try the pigeon or the rabbit.
✉ Just outside Paralimni on the Deryneia Road ☎ 2382 1456

YIANNA MARIE
Splendid location, a little behind the beach.
✉ Fig Tree Bay ☎ 2831 4440

Cafés are a way of life in Cyprus

CYPRUS
where to...

Larnaka & the Southeast

ALWAYS ROOM FOR ONE MORE

No Cypriot restaurateur has been known to turn custom away. The place may be packed, but somehow a space will be created, tables and chairs found, with the tablecloth going on almost faster than the eye can see.

AGÍA NAPA

ARCADIA (££)
Family restaurant serving good meze, steaks and grills.
✉ 1 Belogianni Street
☎ 2372 1479   🕐 Daily

HOKKAIDO (££)
High-quality Japanese food. Smart interior.
✉ 35 Agias Mavris Street
☎ 2372 1505   🕐 Daily

LIMELIGHT TAVERNA (££)
Excellent reputation for Greek dishes and grills.
✉ Liperti Street
☎ 2372 1650   🕐 Daily

VASSOS FISH HARBOUR (££)
Very popular restaurant and rightly so, with excellent seafood. Near the harbour.
☎ 2372 1884   🕐 Daily

LARNAKA

ALEXANDER (£)
Good if you are on a tight budget as the food is excellent and the service is friendly.
✉ 102 Athinon Avenue
☎ 2465 5544   🕐 Daily

CASA MIA (££)
Really good Italian food in pleasant surroundings.
✉ 14 Okeanias Street, Dhekalia Road opposite Palm Beach Hotel   ☎ 2464 4574
🕐 Daily

DEJA-VU (££)
Smart place that is best for lunch as the dinner menu is limited.
✉ 52 Athinon Avenue
☎ 2465 1503   🕐 Daily

DIONYSSOS FISH TAVERN (££)
On the sea front this restaurant has survived the test of time with its excellent seafood.
✉ 78 Ankara Street
☎ 2465 3658   🕐 Daily

KANTARA (££)
In new and impressive premises. The well-prepared and presented food is always good.
✉ 2 Salaminas, Dhekalia Road, opposite Karpasiana Hotel
☎ 2464 7000   🕐 Daily

1900 ART CAFÉ (£)
Local cuisine, home-baked sweets, and herbs in restored old house with very colourful and unusual interior.
✉ Stassinou 6   ☎ 2465 3027
🕐 Wed–Mon 6–12

PAPARAZZI (££)
The excellent food is complemented by the pleasant atmosphere.
✉ 35 Athinon Avenue
☎ 2465 3988   🕐 Daily

PROTARAS

CONSTANTIA (££)
Family restaurant in a pleasant setting. Extensive menu.
✉ Konnos, near Cape Gkeko by the roadside   ☎ 2383 1946
🕐 Daily in summer

YIANNA MARIE (££)
Does breakfast, lunch and dinner and it's all rather good. The location is marvellous, just set back from the beach.
✉ Fig Tree Bay, north end
☎ 2381 4440   🕐 Daily

Limassol & the South

LIMASSOL

ANDREW'S PLACE (££)

Varied choice of dishes with quality food and service.

✉ 54 Georgiou A Potamos Germasogeia, west of Apollonia Hotel ☎ 2532 1443 ⏱ Daily

BAROLO (£££)

This converted old house with a garden is a delightful place to enjoy some quality food.

✉ 248 Agia Andreou Street ☎ 2576 0767 ⏱ Daily

FIESTA (££)

Enjoy the beautifully cooked dishes right by the sea.

✉ Georgiou A, opposite Oasis Lunar Park, Potamos Germasogeia ⏱ Daily

LADAS OLD HARBOUR FISH RESTAURANT (££)

The fish is straight from the boats in the adjacent harbour. It reaches your plate with the minimum of delay. It's been here for 50 years.

✉ Old Harbour ☎ 2536 5760 ⏱ Daily

LA MER (£)

A good place for lunch if you have just done the Limassol walk (► 15).

✉ 28th October Street, just west of the Municipal Gardens ☎ 2535 6095 ⏱ Daily

MAMAS (£££)

It is a pleasure to eat here. The menu is extensive and a high professional standard is maintained throughout.

✉ Kanika Panorama Court,

Amathountas Avenue, towards Elena Beach Hotel ☎ 2532 3433 ⏱ Daily

MEZE TAVERN REATAURANT (££)

This family restaurant serves lovely Greek food, including excellent meze.

✉ 209 Agiou Andreou Street ☎ 2536 7333 ⏱ Mon–Sat 12–2, 6–11

PALLIO VARKA (££)

In an interesting old building with a varied menu, including excellent Greek dishes.

✉ 1 Vasilisis Street, opposite the castle ☎ 2534 7171 ⏱ Daily

PRIMA ITALIAN RESTAURANT (££)

Modern and colourful. The place for well-presented Italian fare.

✉ 139 Agiou Andreou Steet ☎ 2576 3076 ⏱ Daily

REBECCA'S (£)

There are two TV screens but you hardly notice them and the food is excellent and reasonably priced. Free drink and fruit included.

✉ Amathountas Avenue, east of Arsinoe Hotel ☎ 2531 5345 ⏱ Daily

PISSOURI

BUNCH OF GRAPES INN (££)

The building is splendid and unique. The extensive menu features a blend of traditional Cypriot dishes with the best of British and French cuisine.

✉ Pissouri village ☎ 2522 1275 ⏱ Daily

CARTE BLANCHE

All attempts will be made to satisfy the faddiest of clients. The menu may include every wonderful item of Greek or Turkish cuisine, but if the customer wants egg and chips or something more obscure, the constituents will be procured, cooked and served with the same flourish as would befit the à la carte menu.

Pafos & the West

HIPPO KEBABS

It is thought that when the first settlers came to Cyprus 11,000 years ago they found a ready supply of meat in the form of the pygmy hippopotamus. Although quite agile, it appears that the pig-sized animal was no match for hungry human hunters, who systematically drove it to extinction.

PAFOS

ARGO (££)

Their claim to produce the best meze in town seems eminently reasonable after you have sampled it.

✉ Pafos Afroditis Street, Kato Pafos ☎ 2623 3327
🕐 Daily

DEEP BLUE (££)

Well designed restaurant with a modern nautical feel. Excellent seafood.

✉ 12 Pafos Afroditis Street, Kato Pafos ☎ 2681 8015
🕐 Mon–Sat 6–11

GINA'S PLACE (££)

Bistro-café and wine bar serving gourmet sandwiches and salads with superior imported wines. An adjacent delicatessen counter stocks a wide range of foods.

✉ 23 Agiou Antoniou Street, Kato Pafos ☎ 2693 8017
🕐 Mon–Sat 9.30–9

KINGS APHRODITE RESTAURANT (££)

Greek restaurant offering excellent souvlakia, suckling pig and all the usual Greek fare. Music on Friday night.

✉ Tomb of the Kings Road, 300m after the traffic lights, Kato Pafos ☎ 2694 1917
🕐 Daily

LA PIAZZA (££)

Top-quality Italian food.

✉ 11–12 Alkminis Road,, Kato Pafos ☎ 2681 9921
🕐 Daily

LA PLACE ROYALE (££)

Splendidly terraced with a modern, working waterfall – ideal for a relaxing half hour.

✉ Poseidonos Avenue, Kato Pafos ☎ 2693 3995
🕐 Daily

MOULIA 1 FISH AND CHIPS (£)

Claims to sell the best fish and chips on Cyprus.

✉ 3–4 Leda Street, Kato Pafos ☎ 2693 7101 🕐 Daily

OKIO (£)

Terrific view of the harbour. Sandwiches and crêpes.

✉ Poseidonos Avenue, Kato Pafos ☎ 2622 1901
🕐 Daily

TA MPAVIA (££)

Well-designed and in a good position by the sea. The food is pretty good too.

✉ Poseidonos Avenue, Kato Pafos ☎ 2694 1558 🕐 Daily

POLIS AREA

CENTRAL POINT (£)

A good lunch stop. Prompt service and modest prices.

✉ Polis Square ☎ 2632 1800 🕐 Daily

FINIKAS (££)

Ideal for al fresco dining with a varied menu.

✉ Off the south side of Polis Square ☎ 2632 3403
🕐 Daily

SEAFARE RESTAURANT (££)

The proprietor is charming and the seafood is second to none. The wonderful harbour setting is a bonus.

✉ Latsi harbour, west of Polis ☎ 2632 2274 🕐 Daily

Nicosia & the High Troodos

NICOSIA

EREDOS (££)
In the old city by the Ömeriyeh mosque, this is a reminder of an older Cyprus. There is Cypriot food and occasional Greek music.
✉ Patriarchou Grigoriou ☎ 2275 2250 ⏱ Daily

FINIKAS (££)
Excellent Greek restaurant.
✉ 51 Ledras Street ☎ 2266 0060 ⏱ Daily

IL PAESANO (£££)
Fromagerie, delicatessen, bakery, food hall, wine and beer cellar, brasserie and take away. Parking.
✉ 8A Stassinou Avenue, 200m east of Eleftherias Square ☎ 2276 4430 ⏱ Mon–Sat 9–9

KOSTIS TAVERNA (££)
In a quiet backwater, away from the noisy traffic. Varied menu.
✉ Erini Building, 31 Evagorou Avenue ☎ 2267 0904 ⏱ Daily

PERI OREXEOS (£)
The full Greek Cypriot experience, city style. Note the brown paper table coverings and unusual floor finish.
✉ 4–6 Themistokli Dervi Street ☎ 2268 0608 ⏱ Daily

SITIO (££)
Sit with the beautiful people and watch the world go by at this café/restaurant. The cuisine is international with a light Mediterranean touch.
✉ Makarioos Avenue/Hera Street ☎ 2245 8610 ⏱ Daily

1200 GRILL (££)
Specialises in grilled meat dishes.
✉ Stassinou Avenue/Arnaldas Street ☎ No phone ⏱ Daily

PLATRES

PSILIO DENDRO (££)
The grilled trout is good, as you might expect at a trout farm. The large, popular restaurant is hidden in a valley.
✉ Main Troodos–Limassol road, by the track to Kaledonian Falls ☎ 2542 1350 ⏱ Daily

TO ANOI (££)
Family tavern serving good local fare with a magnificent view over the southern Troodos.
✉ Platres centre ☎ 2542 2900 ⏱ Daily

YIOLANDEL (££)
The paint may be fading but the 30-dish Sunday buffet is excellent, the home-made cakes are delicious, and the proprietors, Akis and Nitsa, give thier guests a sincere welcome.
✉ 3B Makarios Street, near Pentelli Hotel ☎ 2542 1720 ⏱ Daily

TRIMIKLINI

JOHN'S RESTAURANT (££)
Good value with some wonderful dishes and equally wonderful views over the valley.
✉ Trimiklini ☎ 2543 2212 ⏱ Daily

NINETEENTH-CENTURY FARE
'The principal food of the Cypriotes consists of olives, beans, bread and onions' wrote Sir Samuel Baker in *Cyprus as I Saw It* in 1879. These days a wider range of fare is available, although the olive remains ubiquitous.

The North

SKEWER CUISINE

Kebab is a big favourite with the locals. On a summer evening in the suburbs the air is redolent with smouldering charcoal and slowly cooking meat on long skewers. The result is not normally less than delicious for the Cypriots are well practised in this culinary art.

FAMAGUSTA (GAZIMAĞUSA) AREA

AKDENIZ (£)
Lively and popular with the locals. The seafood is delicious.
✉ Just north of Salamis Bay Hotel ☎ 378 8277
◉ Daily

CYPRUS GARDENS (£)
The restaurant's reputation derives from its excellent seafood and chicken dishes.
✉ Cyprus Gardens Complex, Boğaz ◉ Daily

CYPRUS HOUSE (££)
This old village house is decorated in 1930s' style. Gourmets must try it out – don't miss the mouth-watering local delicacies.
✉ Polat Paşa Bulvari, opposite post office ☎ 366 4845 ◉ Lunch and dinner, closed Sun

ERICH'S PUB (£)
Traditional pub food and pints of Gold Fassi lager.
✉ Salamis Road ☎ 366 6214 ◉ Daily from 9AM

KAMALIN'IN YERI (£££)
Fish is the mainstay but the kebabs and meze are also delicious.
✉ Mağusa Boğasi ☎ 371 2515 ◉ Daily

MR LI'S (£)
The Long Beach Country Club is an exclusive establishment in a superb setting by the beach. Mr Li serves Chinese and Malaysian food in lavish surroundings.
✉ Long Beach Country Club, Yeni Iskele ☎ 378 8282
◉ Daily noon–midnight

GÜSELYURT (MORFOU) AREA

ISKELE (££)
Menu includes seafood and vegetable meze. Live music at the weekend.
✉ Güzelyurt centre
☎ 714 2099 ◉ Daily

LIMAN FISH AND CHIPS (£)
Simple menu and another claim as the best for fish in Cyprus. it is certainly a contender.
✉ Gemikonaği ☎ 727 7579
◉ Daily

SOLI INN (£)
Good stopping-off place en route to the ruins of Soli and Vouni. Menu of meze, kebabs, kalamari and fish.
✉ West side of Gemikonaği, west of Güzelyurt ☎ 727 7575
◉ Daily

KYRENIA (GIRNE) & SURROUNDING AREA

ALI PAŞA (£)
Ali, a funny eccentric, welcomes visitors Basil Fawlty style. The taverna overlooks the sea and serves Greek, Turkish and some English dishes.
✉ Lapta, near Celebrity Hotel
☎ 821 8942
◉ Daily from 8PM

ALTINKAYA 2 (££)
A rich variety of seafood in addition to the Turkish and English dishes.
✉ Osanköy, towards Beylerbeyi (Bellapais) ☎ 815 500
◉ Daily, lunch and dinner

ANTIS TAVERN (££)
Excellent local food, lively

atmosphere and live music.

✉ Kyrenia– Karaoğlanoğlu road ☎ 822 2256 ⏰ Daily

BAMBOO (££)

Very good fresh fish. The house speciality is charcoal-grilled steak.

✉ Alsancak, on the road to Deniz Kizi Hotel ☎ 821 8091 ⏰ Daily

CHINESE HOUSE (££)

As the name suggests, traditional Chinese food.

✉ Kyrenia– Karaoğlanoğlu road ☎ 815 2130 ⏰ Dinner daily

COURTYARD INN (££)

This popular restaurant, with its country pub atmosphere, is run by expatriates from the UK. Try the spinach and apricot borek suffed with pâté and prawns. Also serves bar snacks. The roast on Sunday is good.

✉ Karakum village, about 2km east of Kyrenia ☎ 815 3343 ⏰ Daily

THE CROW'S NEST (££)

Pub and restaurant. Cosy atmosphere and open-plan kitchen. The menu embraces Turkish and continental cuisine.

✉ Karaman ☎ 822 2567 ⏰ Daily

EFENDI'S HOUSE (££)

Intimate is a good description for this restaurant tucked away in the Kyrenia back streets. It is popular and reservation is advisable if you'd like to sample the Cypriot and Turkish cuisine.

✉ 6 Kamal Paşa Road, Kyrenia ☎ 815 1149 ⏰ Daily 11.30–2.30, 7.30

GRAPEVINE (££)

International cuisine.

✉ Nicosia Road, Kyrenia ☎ 815 2496 ⏰ 11ᴀᴍ–midnight. Closed Sun

GULER'S FISH RESTAURANT (££)

Overlooks a cove by the shore. Many of the locals claim that the best fish in Kyrenia is served here.

✉ Kyrenia, to the west by the Serif Hotel Apartments ☎ 822 2718 ⏰ Daily

HARBOUR CLUB (£££)

Splendid view over the harbour. French cuisine, first-class seafood and many typical Turkish dishes.

✉ Kyrenia Harbour (near castle) ☎ 815 2211 ⏰ Closed Tue lunch

HILARION VILLAGE RESTAURANT (££)

Tasty local dishes on the rarefied heights of the Kyrenia hills.

✉ Karmi ☎ 822 2574 ⏰ Daily

JASHAN (£££)

Indian cuisine and excellent service. Booking is advisable.

✉ Karmi Road, Edremit village ☎ 822 2514 ⏰ Daily from 5pm

LE JARDIN (£££)

Fine cuisine in romantic setting with bar. Reservations are advisable.

✉ Karakum, east of Kyrenia ☎ 824 4398 ⏰ Closed Tue

MANNERS MAKETH MAN

'Do not start to eat before your elders. Always begin your meal by saying grace and eat with your right hand. Do not produce a knife at the table and do not strip a bone clean, do not be too voracious and do not slouch. Do not blow with your mouth over hot food. Eat in a measured manner, for a person should always eat and drink little.' Eleventh-century Turkish etiquette instructions.

The North

LEMON TREE (££)
Excellent Turkish Cypriot menu including stuffed pastries, grilled fish and meat plus a good meze.
✉ Çatalköy Road, 5km east of Kyrenia ☎ 815 4045
🕐 Daily

LEVANT (££)
Hotpots cooked in clay, fondue by prior booking.
✉ Karaman ☎ 822 2559
🕐 Lunch 12–3, tea/cakes 3–5, dinner 7. Closed Tue

MIRABELLE RESTAURANT (££)
Good international cuisine. Live music on Thursday.
✉ 1km outside Kyrenia on Karakum road ☎ 815 7390
🕐 7–10.30. Closed Mon

MOUNTAIN HOUSE (££)
Mixed Turkish and European cuisine.
✉ Beylerbeyi (Bellapais) Road, Kyrenia ☎ 815 3881
🕐 Daily Mon–Fri, Sat lunch only. Closed Sun

NIAZI'S RESTAURANT (££)
Excellent meat dishes; the kebabs are superb.
✉ West of the harbour, opposite Dome Hotel, Kyrenia
☎ 815 2160 🕐 Daily

OLD MILOS (£)
Traditional food in a lovely setting. Live bands play Wednesday, Friday and Saturday.
✉ Alsancak ☎ 821 8939
🕐 Daily

PINARBASI CINAR (££)
Meet friendly villagers and try the original village cuisine.
✉ Pinarbasi ☎ 834 6684
🕐 Daily

PLANTERS BAR AND BISTRO (££)
Splendid colonial house with palm trees. First class à la carte menu.
✉ Western end of Karaoğlanoğlu, approx 4.5km west of Kyrenia on main road
☎ 822 2219
🕐 Daily 10.45–2.45, 6.45PM–1AM

RAFTERS PUB AND BISTRO(££)
Snack and bistro menu to suit all appetites. Special requests cooked to order but notice required. Booking advisable.
✉ Ozanköy Road, 4km east of Kyrenia ☎ 815 2946
🕐 6–1, Sun from 12. Closed Thu

SET ITALIAN RESTAURANT (£)
Superb courtyard setting with lovely trees. Perfect for a candle-lit dinner.
✉ Caferpasa, Kyrenia, near mosque on first back street behind harbour
☎ 815 2336 🕐 Daily

ST TROPEZ (£££)
Excellent French cuisine in a good setting.
✉ On main road just east of Alsancak ☎ 821 8324
🕐 From 7.30PM. Closed Mon

TREE OF IDLENESS (££)
Fish and kebab dishes and Turkish Cypriot *meze*. Live music Saturday. Courtesy shuttle to hotels in Kyrenia.
✉ Beylerbeyi (Bellapais)
☎ 815 3380 🕐 Daily

VALLEY VIEW RESTAURANT (££)

The menu is impressive: daily fresh fish and seafood, kebab, chicken dishes, meze, and more.

✉ Yani/Çatalköy ☎ 868 7070 ⊕ Daily

VERANDA (££)

Seaside restaurant serving local and international cuisine. Booking advisable.

✉ Sebit Ridvan Street, eastern end of Karaoğlanoğlu ☎ 822 2034 ⊕ Closed Mon

YAMA RESTAURANT (££)

Over 30 kinds of meze are along with fish specials.

✉ Kervamsaray, Karaoğlanoğlu ☎ 822 2888 ⊕ Daily

ZIYA RESTAURANT (££)

Good meze and the best fresh fish.

✉ Çatalköy ☎ 824 402

NORTH NICOSIA

BOGHIJALIAN (££)

Much frequented by locals to enjoy a cuisine that embraces the best Turkish dishes.

✉ Arapahemet ☎ 228 0700 ⊕ Daily

CAFE LEBANON (££)

The pastries and cakes are probably as good as any in Nicosia, north or south.

✉ Mehmet Akif Cadessi ☎ No telephone ⊕ Daily

CALIFORNIAN RESTAURANT (££)

The chef is a master of grilled meat dishes.

✉ Dereböyu ☎ 227 6938 ⊕ Daily

GUNEYDOGU KEBAB HOUSE (£)

Small lunch place backing onto the Green Line.

✉ Short distance from Bedestan ☎ 228 1271 ⊕ Daily, lunch only

KIBRIS ASHEVI (CYPRUS KITCHEN) (£)

The pot roast from the clay oven outside is very satisfactory but must be ordered well in advance. The menu includes many other Cypriot dishes.

✉ 39A Ataturk Caddesi ☎ 223 2751 ⊕ Daily

MUSIC BAR (£)

Small pub with jazz some nights. Between 6 and 7pm it is overflowing with young business people.

✉ Bedrettin Demirel Caddesi ☎ No telephone ⊕ Daily

SANDWICH HOUSE (£)

Sandwiches, quiches and cakes all freshly made plus home-made soup.

✉ 101C Mehmet Akif Caddesi ☎ 228 8229 ⊕ 7–7. Closed Sun

SARICIZMELI (£)

One of the best value restaurants in the capital. Select a composite meal from a multitude of trays.

✉ 174 Kyrenia Caddesi ☎ 227 3782 ⊕ Daily

YAKAMOZ (££)

Varied meze and grilled fish, all at modest prices.

✉ Bedrettin Caddesi ☎ 227 1728 ⊕ Daily

ZIR LOCANTA (££)

Small restaurant with good local dishes.

✉ Istanbul Caddesi ☎ 714 3064 ⊕ Daily, dinner

Larnaka & the Southeast

AGÍA NAPA

AENEAS (£££)
The hotel is close to the beach of Nissi Bay. Low-rise buildings surround a large swimming lagoon, set among pleasant gardens.
✉ Nissi Avenue ☎ 2372 4000; www.aeneas.com.cy

ANMARIA HOTEL (£££)
A relatively pleaceful location with gardens that lead down to the beach. Within easy reach of the resort centre.
✉ Nissi Avenue ☎ 2372 2372 3100

DOME HOTEL (££)
A large four-star hotel overlooking two beaches. Lush gardens surround a good-sized swimming pool. Refurbished 2004.
✉ Makronissos ☎ 2372 1006; www.domehotel.com.cy

GRECIAN BAY HOTEL (££)
Directly overlooking the bay, this hotel has an wide choice of facilities including poolside dining and cool mimosa gardens.
✉ 32 Kriou Nerou Avenue ☎ 2384 2400; www.grecian.com.cy

NISSI BEACH HOTEL (££)
The first hotel to be built at this little bay, it stands next to the beach. The facilities are extensive.
✉ Nissi Avenue ☎ 2372 1021; www.nissi-beach.com

OLYMPIC LAGOON RESORT (££)
The hotel is west of the town and built around a lagoon of rocky waterfalls and whirlpools. It is 100m to the beach.
✉ Xylophagou/Agía Napa Road 3km to resort centre ☎ 2372 2500; www.kanikahotels.com

LARNAKA

LORDOS BEACH HOTEL (££)
Designed and run by the Lordos Group. By the sands of Larnaka Bay, it is 7km from the town.
✉ Dhekalia Road ☎ 2464 7444; www.lordos.com/cy

LOUIS PRINCESS BEACH (££)
The 138 rooms at this complex are arranged around a good-sized pool and terraces. Next to the beach.
✉ Dhekalia Road, 6km from the town ☎ 2464 5500

SUN HALL HOTEL (£)
Very close to the beach and well placed for exploring old Larnaka. The outdoor pool is heated in chillier months.
✉ Athinon Avenue ☎ 2465 3341

PROTARAS

PALLINI (£)
These hotel apartments are right on splendid Fig Tree Bay, although away from the main town.
✉ Fig Tree Bay ☎ 3383 1400

PERNERA BEACH HOTEL (££)
A good retreat situated mid-way betwen Protaras and Paralimni (about 3km to each).
✉ Pernera ☎ 2383 1011

Limassol & the South

LIMASSOL

AMATHUS BEACH (£££)
Opulent and with fine gardens, it is situated by the shore at the eastern end of the tourist strip.
✉ Amathous Avenue
☎ 2583 2000;
www.amathushotel.com

ATLANTICA BAY (££)
In an elevated position near ancient Amathous.
✉ Amathous Avenue
☎ 2563 4070;
www.atlanticahotels.com

CURIUM PALACE (£)
An older style hotel and one which has maintained high standards. The antique furniture and friendly owner add to the atmosphere. The dining options are first class.
✉ 2 Byron Street
☎ 2536 3121/2589 1100

FOUR SEASONS (£££)
The hotel enjoys a good reputation. Interior finishes are high quality, and the swimming pool is excellent. Thalassotherapy and seaweed treatments are among the facilities.
✉ Amathous Avenue
☎ 2585 8000;
www.fourseasons.com.cy

LE MERIDIEN (£££)
Excellent in every respect including sumptuous well-planned rooms and lawns that sweep down to the shore. Residents-only operations means privacy and exclusive use of all the facilities.
✉ Old Limassol–Nicosia road
☎ 2586 2000;
www.lemeridien-cyprus.com

MIRAMARE BAY RESORT (££)
The hotel was built long before Limassol's coastal strip became a continuous ribbon of development. Service is excellent.
✉ Amerikanas Street, Potamos Germasogeia ☎ 2588 8100;
www.miramare.com.cy

SUNSMILE HOTEL APARTMENTS (£)
A good base if you're on a budget. The apartments are self-catering but basic. Good cheap meals are available in the dining room. Moderate-sized pool. Friendly staff.
✉ 9 Xenaphanous Street
☎ 2532 0700; email:
Sunsmile@cytanet.com.cy

PISSOURI

BUNCH OF GRAPES (£)
A restored inn with 11 rooms and a pleasant courtyard. Quite different to modern hotels.
✉ Pissouri village
☎ 2522 1275

HYLATIO TOURIST VILLAGE (£)
These pleasing apartments and studios with a pool do not have a sea view but the beach is only a short walk away. Car hire would enhance a quiet holiday.
✉ Pissouri Beach area
☎ 2522 2701

PISSOURIANA PLAZA APARTMENTS (£)
Reasonably spacious apartments with pool. Tremendous view.
✉ Pissouri village
☎ 2522 1027;
www.pissouriana.com

MOSQUITO HUNTING

Visitors susceptible to mosquitoes should ensure they patrol their rooms before retiring. Any idle insect on the wall should be dispatched. Modern sprays are suitable for the squeamish. If they are not available a suitably thick paperback will prove an adequate substitute. A few sleepless nights from the whine of the mosquito are a powerful incentive to perfect the technique.

RURAL HIDEAWAYS

Agro-tourism is the new buzz word for the Cypriot tourist authorities. The plan is to help proprietors renovate traditional houses in the villages to attract a different kind of tourist and spare the remainder of Cyprus the ravages of intensive development.

Pafos & the West, Nicosia & the High Troodos

NO ROOM ON THE ISLAND

In July 1992 Cyprus was said to be full. Leading holiday firms met the Cyprus Tourism authorities to discuss fears that the island would burst at the seams during August. The crisis was brought about by an increase in tourists of 120 per cent.

MONASTIC RETREATS

Until quite recently the monasteries would always find a bed for a traveller. Today the monks are less obliging.

PAFOS

AGAPINOR (£)
Well appointed rooms (73) plus restaurant and coffee shop. Remarkable views.
✉ 22–28 Nikodemos Mylonas Street, Pafos ☎ 2693 3926; www.agapinorhotel.com.cy

AKAMANTHEA TOURIST VILLAGE (££)
Excellent small complex in wonderful surroundings. Self catering with lots of facilities, a swimming pool and a central area.
✉ Latsi, near Polis ☎ 2632 3500; www.akamanthea.com

ALMYRA (£££)
Enviable shore location 600m from the harbour.
✉ Poseidon Avenue, Kato Pafos ☎ 2688 3300; www.thanoshotels.com

ALOE (£££)
Enviable shore location 600m from the harbour.
✉ Poseidon Avenue, Kato Pafos ☎ 2688 4000; www.aloe-hotel.com.cy

ANNABELLE (£££)
A renowned luxury hotel in a prime position in town.
✉ Poseidon Avenue, Kato Pafos ☎ 2693 8333; www.thanoshotels.com

NICOSIA

AVEROF (£)
Traditional hotel in a quiet area just outside the city.
✉ 19 Averof Street, Nicosia ☎ 2277 3447

CASTELLI HOTEL (££)
Conviently close to the commercial and historic districts of Nicosia. International style.
✉ 38 Ouzounian Street, Nicosia ☎ 2271 2812

CLASSIC (££)
Just within the walled city, this is convenient for the central area of Nicosia.
✉ 94 Regaena Street, Nicosia ☎ 2266 4006; www.classic.com.cy

CLEOPATRA (££)
A popular hotel, in the new town with luxurious rooms and six suites.
✉ 8 Florina Street, Nicosia ☎ 2267 1000; email cleotel@cleopatra.com.cy

HILTON CYPRUS (£££)
Nicosia's most expensive hotel, a prestigious establishment on elevated ground on the south side of the city complete with large pool and extensive facilities.
✉ Makarios Avenue, ☎ 2237 7777; www.hilton.com

PLATRES

CHURCHILL PINEWOOD (£)
This cosy hotel with 49 rooms is close to Prodromos, the highest village in Cyprus and quite remote, but ideal for exploring the Troodos.
✉ Prodromos/Pedoulas ☎ 2295 2211; email: pinewood@churchill.com.cy

EDELWEISS (£)
A small pleasant hotel.
✉ 5 Spyroni Kypriano Street, Platres ☎ 2542 1335; www.edelweisshotel.com.cy

The North

FAMAGUSTA

BLUE SEA HOTEL (£)
This hotel by the sea is ideal for an overnight stay in Karpasia. Simple rooms. Good fish dinner.
✉ 5km southeast of Dipkarpaz village ☎ 372 2393; email: bluesea@northcyprus.net

MIMOZA (££)
On the water's edge on a sandy beach, near ancient Salamis.
✉ Just north of Salamis ☎ 378 8219; email: mimoza@northcyprus.net

SALAMIS BAY CONTI RESORT (£££)
Large, impressive complex on a fine beach close to the ruins of ancient Salamis. Excellent facilities.
✉ Salamis Bay ☎ 378 8200/8201; www.salamisbayconti.com

NORTH NICOSIA

ROYAL (££)
Modern hotel with extensive facilities including indoor pool, Turkish bath, sauna and massage centre.
✉ 19 Kemal Asik Caddesi ☎ 228 7621; email: royalhotel@northcyprus.net

SARAY HOTEL (££)
Excellent central location for shopping and sightseeing. High standards make this a popular venue. The rooftop restaurant balcony offers terrific views across Nicosia.
✉ Ataturk Meydani ☎ 228 3115; email: saray@northcyprus.net

KYRENIA (GIRNE) & THE WEST

BRITISH HOTEL (£)
Good Kyrenia harbour location. Great views from the restaurant roof terrace. Ask about the VIP service.
✉ Kordonboyu, west end of harbour ☎ 815 2240; email: british@northcyprus.net

DOME HOTEL (££)
The longest established hotel in Cyprus occupies a rocky outcrop near the harbour. A seawater pool is built into an enclosure to the front of the hotel.
✉ Kordonboyu Caddesi ☎ 815 2453; email: thedome@kktc.net

DORANA (£)
Near the shopping area and harbour but quiet.
✉ 143 Ziya Riski Avenue, west of the harbour ☎ 815 3521; email: dorana@northcyprus.net

LA HOTEL (££)
Low-rise hotel around a good size pool. A pleasant beach is close by, reached through an underpass to the road.
✉ Lapta, west of Kyrenia ☎ 821 8981; email: info@lahotel.net

PIA BELLA (££)
About a 20-minute walk to the harbour. The garden annex has superior rooms.
✉ 14 Iskendurun Avenue, Kyrenia ☎ 815 5321; email: piabella@kktc.net

SOLI INN (£)
Seaside hotel near the ruins of Soli, in Güzelyurt Bay.
✉ Gemikonagi ☎ 727 7575; email: soliinn@northcyprus.net

PICTURESQUE PLUMBING

The older Cypriot hotels are known for their erratic plumbing, quite apart from the fact that the drains cannot cope with toilet paper, taps which have been put on the wrong way round and showers which seem to have been adapted from water cannons are not uncommon.

73

Souvenir, Handicrafts & Leather

SHOPPING HOURS

May–Sep, Mon–Fri 8–1, 4–7, Sat 8–1; Oct–Apr, Mon–Fri 8–1, 2:30–5:30
Shops in tourist areas, north and south, will stay open later.

SILK MAKING

Cyprus had, until recently, a great tradition of silk making going back to the Byzantine period. The warm coastal climate and abundance of mulberry trees were ideal for the silkworms and the weaving of silk became a significant cottage industry. Production declined when rural areas turned to the cultivation of lemon groves instead.

LARNAKA & THE SOUTHEAST

Laïki Geitonia (traditional quarter) at the south end of Zenon Kiteios Street has a few shops of interest although type and ownership change regularly. About 750m to the south on Bozkourt and Ak Deniz streets are a number of pottery shops.

CYPRUS HANDICRAFT SERVICE

This is a Ministry of Commerce and Industry initiative and the shop has all the traditional Cypriot crafts including Lefkara lace, leather goods, woven cotton, silverware, baskets and wood-carved items.
✉ 6 Kosma Lysioti Street, Larnaka ☎ 2463 0327

EMIRA POTTERY

Handmade pots of all types.
✉ 13 Mehmet Ali Street, Larnaka ☎ 2462 3952

FOTONI'S POTTERY

✉ 28 Boz Kourt, Larnaka ☎ 2465 0304

KORNOS VILLAGE

Terracotta pottery is still produced here in the same way as 2,000 years ago.

LIOPETRI AND XYLOFAGOU VILLAGES

Traditional basket-making.

MARY'S TOURIST SHOP

Leather goods, Lefkara lace, handmade souvenirs.
✉ 26 Zenon Kiteous Street, Larnaka ☎ 2465 4393

LIMASSOL & THE SOUTH

ARTOUCH

Paintings, sculptures, ceramics and hand-crafted jewellery.
✉ Agios Andreou Street, Limassol ☎ 2576 2660

CYPRUS HANDICRAFT SERVICE

Traditional Cypriot handicrafts.
✉ 25 Themidos Street, Limassol ☎ 2530 5118

HOUSE OF LACE

Large selection of Lefkara lace.
✉ West end of Agios Andreou Street, Limassol

LEFKARA VILLAGE (► 49)

A wide range of silverware and lace products are on sale here. Check that you are offered the genuine article and not an import.

SCAFARI 2

Interesting copper and leather products.
✉ 46 Agios Andreou Street, Limassol

SEA SPONGE EXHIBITION CENTRE

Natural beauty products, including soaps and loofahs.
✉ Old Port, Limassol

PAFOS & THE WEST

CYPRUS HANDICRAFT CENTRE

A wide selection of traditional Cypriot crafts.
✉ 64 Apostolou Pavlou Avenue, Kato Pafos ☎ 2694 0243

FYTI VILLAGE

The villagers produce fine woven cloth, especially embroidered curtains.

MAVRIS LEATHER HOUSE

Leather garmets off the peg or made to measure.
✉ 5 Dionysos Street, Kato Pafos ☎ 2693 5646

MOSIACS PLAZA

Unique gifts and souvenirs in gold and silver, plus mineral and gemstone items. Also a selection of leather goods.
✉ Harbour, Kato Pafos
☎ 2681 9999

NICOSIA & THE HIGH TROODOS

CYPRUS HANDICRAFT CENTRE

Promotes and sells Cypriot handicrafts.
✉ 186 Athalassa Avenue, Nicosia ☎ 2230 5024

FOINI VILLAGE

A reputation for its pottery encourages enthusiasts to make the long journey to this remote area.

LAÏKI GEITONEA

Refurbished and traffic-free tourist area of the walled city housing some craft shops.
✉ East of Eleftheria Square, Nicosia

LEVENTIS MUSEUM GIFT SHOP

Reproductions of historical artefacts including some attractive jewellery.
✉ Ippokratous Street, Nicosia (walled city)

MICHALIAS STUDIO

Ceramic tile murals, street numbers, coasters.
✉ 33 Lefkonos Street, Nicosia (walled city) ☎ 2275 3900

MOUFFLON BOOKSHOP

Extensive selection of books about Cyprus.
✉ 1 Sofouli Street, Nicosia (walled city) ☎ 2265 5155

MOUTOULLAS

Famed for its bottled drinking water, this mountain village also produces fine wooden basins and copper goods.

OMODOS

Souvenir shops abound. The embroidery is well worth seeking out.

THE NORTH

BEYRAMOGLU LTD.

Quality handbags and shoes.
✉ Hurriyet Street, Kyrenia (Girne) ☎ 815 2216

CYPRUS CORNER

Collection of copperware, brass, onyx pieces.
✉ Selimiye Meydani, Nicosia
☎ 227 1519

SENAK SOUVENIR SHOP

Some interesting onyx and copper designs and local pottery, plus carpets.
✉ Harbour by the mosque, Kyrenia (Girne) ☎ 815 2811

TRNC HANDICRAFTS COOPERATIVE LTD.

Local crafts.
✉ 9 Evkaf Is Hani, Kyrenia (Girne) Avenue, Nicosia ☎ 227 1368

BREAKING THE LAW

All Turkish-made products are banned from the Greek part of Cyprus. Shopkeepers who break the law risk two years in prison or a fine of £1,400. In 1995 Body Shop apologised after Turkish-made face flannels were found in one of its shops.

Stores, Arcades & Markets

STORES & ARCADES

SPECTACULAR SAVINGS

Cypriot opticians have spotted a gap in the market and offer special tourist services of a quick turn around for sight tests and spectacles, all provided at a fraction of the cost at home.

LARNAKA & THE SOUTHEAST

FORUM

This modest emporium features well-designed quality goods.
✉ 96–102 Zenon Kiteous, Larnaka ☎ 2465 9200

WOOLWORTH ZENON

A typical store selling everything from records to jewellery to lingerie. It has a food hall and bookshop.
✉ Stratigou Timagia Avenue ☎ 2463 1111

LIMASSOL & THE SOUTH

AGORA

An impressive modern arcade. Some quality clothes and footwear outlets along with a unique jewellery gallery.
✉ Junction of Agios Andreou and Anexartisias Streets, Limassol

ANEXARTISIA SHOPPING STREET

Claims 165 shops. That won't be the case for long but the Street is here to stay and worth a visit.
✉ Anexartisias Street, Limassol

MEDIEVAL ARCADE

Mainly restaurants aand cafés,but including a bookshop.
✉ West end of Agiou Andreou Street, Limassol

WOOLWORTH OLYMPIA

The standard range of department store goods.
✉ 369, 28 October Street ☎ 2559 1133

PAFOS & THE WEST

MOSAICS PLAZA

Relatively small but includes souvenirs, leather and jewellery, plus a cafeteria.
✉ Pafos harbour, Kato Pafos ☎ 2681 9999

WOOLWORTH KINYRAS

A very smart store.
✉ West end of Poseidonos Avenue, Pafos ☎ 2694 7122

NICOSIA & THE HIGH TROODOS

CAPITAL CENTER

This was the first real shopping centre in Cyprus, and is still worth a look.
✉ Makarios Avenue, Nicosia

CITY PLAZA

The basement is for food, while the three upper levels of upmarket shops are dedicated to clothes, shoes and sportswear shops.
✉ Makarios Avenue, Nicosia

DEBENHAMS

Worth a look to compare with UK branches.
✉ 5–15 Makarios Avenue, Nicosia

WOOLWORTH CENTRAL AND WOOLWORTH LEDRA

There are two stores and the one on Makarios Avenue – hardly recognisable as a Woolworth – houses distinctively separate retailers on the vrious floors. One attraction of

the branch in the walled city is the roof restaurant which has remarkable views over Turkish Cypus.
✉ Central: Makarios Avenue, junction with Gigeni Akrita. Ledra: 171–179 Ledras Street, Nicosia
☎ 2559 1133

THE NORTH

EVKAF ISHANI PRECINCT
✉ Kyrenia (Girne) Avenue, Nicosia

GALLERIA ARCADE
Two floors of relatively modern shops.
✉ Arasta Street, Nicosia

MARKETS

LARNAKA & THE SOUTHEAST

MUNICIPAL FRUIT AND VEGETABLE MARKET.
✉ Ermou Street, Larnaka

LIMASSOL & THE SOUTH

CENTRAL MARKET
Fruit and vegetables.
✉ Saripolou Street, Limassol

MUNICIPAL MARKET
✉ Genethliou Mitella Street, Limassol

PAFOS & THE WEST

MUNICIPAL MARKET
Open air stalls selling fruit and vegetables.
✉ Fellahoglou Street, Pafos (old town)

NICOSIA & THE

HIGH TROODOS

MUNICIPAL MARKET
Open air stalls selling fruit and vegetables.
✉ Plateia Dimarchias, Nicosia (walled city)

OPEN AIR MARKET
A splended place to buy fish, fruit and vegetables, all in the shadow of a mosque.
✉ Constanza Bastion, Konstantious Avenue, Nicosia

THE NORTH

COVERED BAZAAR
✉ South side of Selimiye Mosque, Nicosia

COVERED BAZAAR
✉ North end of Canbulat Yolu, Famagusta

OKKES DAYI MARKET
✉ Attaturk Caddesi, Kyrenia

ENTHUSIASTIC SALES PITCH

Cypriot shopkeepers will never admit defeat. If they cannot convince you that the size or colour is just right then your choice will be promised for tomorrow. The promise should not be taken too literally.

Festivals

TRADITIONAL FESTIVALS

The Greek Cypriots have a wealth of traditional festivals and fairs. Many derive from the Greek Orthodox Church, others have pagan origins. Despite this rich heritage the number of events grows. There are now beauty contests, Olympic Day 10-km runs, beer festivals, dog shows and annual exhibitions of coinage.

AGÍA NAPA FESTIVAL (LATE SEPTEMBER)

A weekend of folk music, dance and theatre combined with agricultural exhibitions.

LARNAKA FESTIVAL (JULY)

Dance, theatre and music at the fort and the Municipal Amphitheatre, Artemedos Avenue.
☎ 2465 7745

ANCIENT GREEK DRAMA FESTIVAL (JUNE–AUGUST)

Classical drama staged the amphitheatre at Kourion and other open-air theatres in the area.

LIMASSOL FESTIVAL

Theatre, music and dance events through summer.
☎ 2536 3103

WINE FESTIVAL

First week in September. Music, dance and wine tasting in the Municipal Gardens.

MUNICIPAL THEATRE

Performances by local and international companies.
✉ Museum Street
☎ 2258 5000

PAFOS FESTIVAL

Pafos Municipality organises theatre, music and dance events through the summer at the Odeion amphitheatre and the harbour fort.
☎ 2693 2804

Seminars and other cultural events throughout the year.
✉ Attatürk Cultural Centre, Northern Nicosia

MOVEABLE FEASTS

EASTER

The biggest Greek Orthodox feast. The pre-Lenten Carnival has 10 days of entertainments and feasting, finishing on Green Monday, an occasion for picnics in the country.

APOKREO FESTIVITIES

50 days before Orthodox Easter Sunday: two weeks of fun.

PROCESSION OF AGIOS LAZAROS ICON, LARNAKA

8 days before Orthodox Easter Sunday.

KATAKLYSMOS, FESTIVAL OF THE FLOOD

50 days after Easter Sunday: celebrations in all the seaside towns.

SEKER OR RAMAZAN BAYRAM

A three-day feast at the end of the Ramadan fast.

KURBAN BAYRA

Four days during which lambs are sacrificed and shared with the needy.

Outdoor Activities

ANGLING

Fishing is permitted in numerous dams around the island on purchase of a licence. Licences are available from from the Fisheries Departments:

✉ Piale Pasha Avenue, Larnaca
☎ 2463 4294
✉ Paralimni office
☎ 2382 5934

✉ Limassol Harbour
☎ 2463 4294

✉ Pafos Harbour
☎ 2630 6268

✉ Aiolou, Nicosia
☎ 2280 7861

BIRD WATCHING

Cyprus is on the migration route for birds between Europe and Africa. About 98 species are resident on the island and 200 more regular visitors include 10,000 flamingos which winter on the Salt Lake west of Larnaka.

SOUTH:
CYPRUS ORNITHOLOGICAL SOCIETY.
✉ 4 Kanaris Street, Nicosia
☎ 2242 0703

NORTH:
SOCIETY FOR THE PROTECTION OF BIRDS.
☎ 815 7337

BOWLING (TEN PIN)

CYPRUS BOWLING ASSOCIATION
✉ PO Box 5287, Nicosia
☎ 2235 0085

LARNAKA & THE SOUTHEAST

ROCK 'N' BOWL
✉ Dhekalia Road, Larnaka
☎ 2482 2777 ⏰ Daily 10AM–midnight

VIRTUALITY BOWLING CENTRE
✉ 24 Eleftherias Street, Agia Napa
☎ 23723290 ⏰ Daily 10AM–midnight

LIMASSOL & THE SOUTH

LIMASSOL BOWLING
✉ Argyrokastrou Street, Limassol ☎ 2537 0414
⏰ 2PM–midnight

SPACE BOWLING
✉ 1 Hercules Street, Germasogeia, motorway junction 23 area ☎ 2531 0000
⏰ Daily 10AM–2AM

PAFOS & THE WEST

COKATOOS
✉ Ayiou Antoniou Street, Kato Pafos ☎ 2682 2004 ⏰ Daily 10–2

CYCLING

Cycles can be hired in most resorts. The Cyprus Tourism Organisataion in Nicosia issues an excellent booklet of routes.

CYPRUS CYCLING FEDERATION
✉ PO Box 24572, Nicosia
☎ 2266 3344

LIMASSOL CYCLING CLUB
✉ PO Box 56142, Limassol
☎ 2558 5980

BEHIND THE WHEEL

When driving in Cyprus be aware that road conditions vary dramatically, and suddenly, across the island. Also note that motorists attempting to cross the border will find it very time consuming, due to the extensive formalities in place.

Outdoor Activities

WATER SKIING

Discounts can be negotiated for the promise to turn up every day. However, almost certainly the boat will be broken down, or elsewhere, when it is wanted. In addition an eye should be kept on the time allocation, for mysterious laws of relativity tend to make the driver's watch run faster than the skiers. For further information ➤ 82.

CYPRUS CAR RALLY

This tough event takes place every year and is part of the World Rally Championship. The time is outlined in the championship calendar. For information contact:

CYPRUS AUTOMOBILE ASSOCIATION.
☎ 2231 3233

DIVING

The water temperature varies between 16°C and 27°C. There are diving centres and sub-aqua clubs in all the seaside towns and at various hotels. For information:

SOUTH: CYPRUS FEDERATION OF UNDERWATER ACTIVITIES
✉ PO Box 21503, Nicosia
☎ 2275 4647

NORTH: AMPHORA SCUBA DIVING CENTRE
☎ 851 4924

FOOTBALL

There is an established league structure with pitches in main towns. Successful teams compete regularly in internationals. Grounds are rented out to European clubs for winter training. For further information:

CYPRUS FOOTBALL ASSOCIATION
☎ 2235 2341

GSP STADIUM
Nicosia's impressive ground is ultramodern, seats 26,000 and is used for league and international matches (and athletics).
✉ Junction 6 off the Limassol Highway

TSIRION STADIUM
Hosts major league games.
✉ 5km north of Limassol centre, off A1 highway

GOLF

There are four 18-hole golf courses on the island – all in splendid locations.

PAFOS & THE WEST

APHRODITE HILLS)
✉ North of Pafos
☎ 2531 6560

SECRET VALLEY GOLF CLUB
✉ East of Pafos near, Petra tou Romiou ☎ 2664 2774

TSADA
✉ North of Pafos
☎ 2664 2774

LIMASSOL & THE SOUTH

VIKLA GOLF COURSE
Reasonable green fee for as many rounds as you like.
✉ Vikla, 25km northeast of Limassol, Parekklisia exit from highway ☎ 2562 2894

HANG-GLIDING

LIMASSOL & THE SOUTH

Main area is Kourion (Curium) sea cliffs.

**CYPRUS AIRSPORTS
FEDERATION**
☎ 2233 9771

SOTOS
☎ 9960 6211

THE NORTH

Takes place in the Kyrenia
Hills

**TURKISH AVIATION
FEDERATION**
☎ 856 8363

HORSE RACING

Horse racing takes place
throughout the year in the
Republic.

NICOSIA & THE
HIGH TROODOS

**NICOSIA
RACECOURSE**
✉ St Paul's Street, west of the
city centre ☎ 2278 2727 🕔
Wed and Sat (check times)

HORSE RIDING

**CYPRUS EQUESTRIAN
FEDERATION**
☎ 9967 3333

LARNAKA &
THE SOUTHEAST

MOONSHINE RANCH
✉ Kavo Gkreko Road, opposite
Grecian Bay Hotel, Agía Napa
☎ 9960 5042

LIMASSOL &
THE SOUTH

**AMATHOUS PARK
RIDING SCHOOL**
✉ Near Parekklisia, highway
junction 21
☎ 2560 4109

DRAPIA FARM
✉ Kalavasos, 30km east of
Limassol ☎ 2433 2998

**ELIAS BEACH HORSE
RIDING CENTRE**
✉ Near Parekklisia, 10km east
of Limassol
☎ 2532 6000 ext 317

MOUTTAYIAKI RANCH
✉ Just notth of highway
junction 23, Limassol
☎ 9943 7515

NICOSIA & THE
HIGH TROODOS

NICOSIA RIDING CLUB
✉ Agios Trimithis, 20km
southwest of Nicosia
☎ 9967 1789

There is also riding on
most summer days at
Troodos Square on Mount
Olympus.

PAFOS & THE
WEST

GEORGE'S RANCH
✉ Agios Georgios, 20km north
of Pafos ☎ 2662 1790

**PADDOCKS
EQUESTRIAN CENTRE**
✉ Kissonerga, 10km north of
Pafos ☎ 2693 3358

THE NORTH

TUNAC RIDING CLUB
✉ Karaoglanoglu
☎ 822 2868

SAILING

LARNAKA &
THE SOUTHEAST

**LARNAKA NAUTICAL
CLUB**
☎ 2462 3399

DOUBTFUL DIRECTIONS

Some of the activities listed on
these pages entail trips into
the quieter parts of Cyprus.
The visitor, if lost or doubtful
of the route, should beware of
directions given by villagers.
They will be anxious to please
and in an attempt not to
disappoint may assume an
unjustifiable knowledge.

Outdoor Activities

SHOOTING

Hunting, mainly the shooting of migratory birds, is a common pursuit in the rural areas, much to the despair of environmental groups. Attempts to ban or restrict the annual slaughter have failed to date.

LARNAKA MARINA
Facilities for visiting yachts – very popular, so reserve space well in advance.
☎ 2465 3110/3113

LIMASSOL & THE SOUTH

LIMASSOL NAUTICAL CLUB
☎ 2532 4282

RELAX CATAMARAN CRUISES
☎ 8000 8007

ST RAPHAEL MARINA
✉ Limassol ☎ 2532 1100 Ext 3312

PAFOS & THE WEST

PAFOS NAUTICAL CLUB
☎ 2694 3700

PAFOS SEA CRUISES
☎ 2691 0200

THE NORTH

KYRENIA (GIRNE) HARBOUR
Berthing for Turkish Cypriot boats and craft touring the eastern Mediterrranean.

SHOOTING

CYPRUS SHOOTING SPORTS FEDERATION
General information about all the clubs.
✉ PO Box 12681, 8km southwest of Nicosia
☎ 2248 6673

CYPRUS OLYMPIC SHOOTING RANGE (NICOSIA SPORTING CLUB)
✉ PO Box 22190, Latsia area, 8km southwest of Nicosia
☎ 2248 2660

SKIING

NICOSIA & THE HIGH TROODOS

MOUNT OLYMPUS
The season runs from January until March. Two ski lifts operate in Sun Valley giving runs of about 200m. Other lifts on the north face of the mountain, one 500m long and one of 350m, offer more demanding skiing. Sometimes the conditions allow two cross-country tracks to open. Ski equipment can be hired in Sun Valley.

CYPRUS SKI CLUB
✉ PO Box 22185, Nicosia
☎ 2267 5340

SWIMMING

The extensive coastline offers excellent opportunities for swimmers. Red buoys indicate swimming areas. Most beaches offer safe bathing, but some beaches in the Pafos area can be dangerous in rough weather and warning flags (green safe, yellow caution, red danger) should be heeded. Part of the beach at Kourion, again clearly marked, is also unsafe and should be avoided. There are no private beaches on Cyprus.

LARNAKA & THE SOUTHEAST

LARNAKA PUBLIC BEACH

This is a popular location for swimming with changing facilities and a café on site. Free entry.
- ✉ 10km east of Larnaka
- ☎ 2464 4511

LIMASSOL & THE SOUTH

DHASSOUDI PUBLIC BEACH

Changing facilities and café.
- ✉ 5km east of Limassol
- ☎ 2532 2811

PAFOS & THE WEST

GEROSKIPOU

Changing facilities and café.
- ✉ 3km east of Pafos
- ☎ 2623 4525

TENNIS

There are courts in al the main towns. Contact
CYPRUS TENNIS FEDERATION
- ✉ PO Box 23931,. Nicosia
- ☎ 2266 8041; email
cytennis@spidernet.com.cy

Many of the larger hotels have well laid-out courts.

LIMASSOL & THE SOUTH

ELIAS COUNTRY CLUB
- ✉ Near Parekklisia, Limassol
- ☎ 2532 5000;
www.elaisbeach.cy.net

WATER SPORTS

Parascending, wind surfing, water skiing and banana tows are available fom the main beaches or by the big hotels. Pedalos, canoes and small catamarans can similarly be hired. On some beaches motor boats are available for hire. For catamaran cruises ➤ 80.

WALKING

Midsummer is much too hot for this pastime – even the mountain tempertures prove too high for most people. All walkers should remember that even at high altitude the weather can be very hot and that anyone undertaking a strenous walk or climb should take water with them. Conversely, those walking in winter should realise that many of the mountain are very high and that bad weather is common. Suitably warm clothing is essential. See also page 58.

There are trails across the country designed by Cyprus Tourist Organisation. For information contact the offices listed on page 88.

SKIERS DILEMMA

Skiing enthusiasts have a dilemma. At weekends they need to get to the ski shop early before the best gear is given out, but if there has been overnight snow they will be lucky to get their cars up the last section of Mount Olympus before the snow plough. Another reason for getting on the slopes early is that the snow soon turns to mush in the mid-morning heat – powder snow is a rarity.

CYPRUS
practical matters

BEFORE YOU GO

WHAT YOU NEED

● Required ○ Suggested ▲ Not required	Some countries require a passport to remain valid for a minimum period (usually at least six months) beyond the date of entry – contact their consulate or embassy or your travel agent for details.	UK	Germany	USA	Netherlands	Spain
Passport/National Identity Card		●	●	●	●	●
Visa (➤ 87, Arriving. Regulations can change – check before your visit to Cyprus.)		▲	▲	▲	▲	▲
Onward or Return Ticket, Republic of Cyprus		●	●	●	●	●
Onward or Return Ticket, Northern Cyprus		▲	▲	▲	▲	▲
Health Inoculations		▲	▲	▲	▲	▲
Travel and Health Insurance (➤ 90, Health)		○	○	○	○	○
Driving Licence (national with English translation or International)		●	●	●	●	●
Car Insurance Certificate (if own car)		●	●	●	●	●
Car Registration Document (if own car)		●	●	●	●	●

WHEN TO GO

Coastal Cyprus

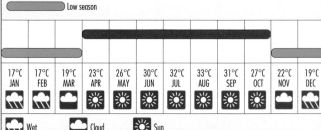

High season

Low season

17°C JAN	17°C FEB	19°C MAR	23°C APR	26°C MAY	30°C JUN	32°C JUL	33°C AUG	31°C SEP	27°C OCT	22°C NOV	19°C DEC

Wet   Cloud   Sun

TIME DIFFERENCES

GMT 12 noon	Cyprus 2PM	Germany 1PM	USA (NY) 7AM	Netherlands 1PM	Spain 1PM

TOURIST OFFICES

In the UK
Cyprus Tourist Office
17 Hanover Street
London W1R 0AA
☎ 020 7569 8800;
ctolon@ctolon.demon
.co.uk

Northern Region of Cyprus
Tourist Information Office
29 Bedford Square
London WC1B 3EG
☎ 020 7631 1920;
info@go-northcyprus.com

In the USA
Cyprus Tourism
Organisation
13 East 40th Street
New York NY 10016
☎ 212/683 5280;
gocyprus@aol.com

Northern Region of Cyprus
Tourist Information Office
1667 K Street, Suite
690, Washington
DC 20006
☎ 202/887 6198
Fax: 202/467 0685

ARRIVING

The national airline, Cyprus Airways (☎ 22663054) operates scheduled flights from Britain and mainland Europe to Larnaka and Pafos. There are no direct flights to North Cyprus, you fly via Turkey for which you need a visa if you intend visiting (check visa requirements).

Larnaka Airport
Kilometres to city centre

5 kilometres

Journey times	
🚇	N/A
🚌	30 minutes
🚗	20 minutes

Ercan Airport
Kilometres to Nicosia

23 kilometres

Journey times	
🚇	N/A
🚌	35 minutes
🚗	15 minutes

MONEY

The currency of the **Republic of Cyprus** is the Cyprus pound (C£), divided into 100 cents. Coins are in denominations of 1, 2, 5, 10, 20 and 50 cents; notes C£1, 5, 10 and 20. The currency of **North Cyprus** is the Turkish lira (TL). Coins are TL100, 500, 1,000, 2,500, 5,000, 10,000, 25,000 and 50,000; notes TL10,000, 20,000, 50,000, 100,000, 250,000, 500,000, 1,000,000 and 5,000,000.

TIME

 Cyprus is two hours ahead of Greenwich Mean Time (GMT+2), but from late March, when clocks are put forward one hour, to late October, summer time (GMT+3) operates.

CUSTOMS

 YES

From another EU country taken into Republic of Cyprus (guide-lines):
800 cigarettes
20 cigars
1kg tobacco,
10 litres of spirits (over 22%),
20 litres of wine of which 60 llitres can be sparkling wine,
110 litres of beer

You should check that these standards apply.

Goods Obtained Duty Free taken into North Cyprus (Limits):
Alcohol (over 22% vol): 1.5L
Wine: 1.5L
Cigarettes: 400 or
Cigarillos: 200 or
Cigars: 100 or
Tobacco: 500gms
Perfume: 100ml
Toilet Water: 100ml

You must be 18 or over to benefit from the alcohol and tobacco allowances.

NO

Drugs, firearms, ammunition, offensive weapons, obscene material, unlicensed animals, fruit, nuts, vegetables, cut flowers, bulbs or seeds.

CONSULATES

UK (British
High Commission)
2286 1100 (RoC)
228 3861(NC)

Germany
(Embassy)
2245 1145 (RoC)
227 5161 (NC)

USA
(Embassy)
22776400 (RoC)
225 2240 (NC)

Netherlands
(Consulate)
2586 7240 (RoC)

TOURIST OFFICES

Republic of Cyprus
- Cyprus Tourism Organisation
  PO Box 24535
  CY 1390 Nicosia
  ☎ 2269 1100; email:
  cytour@cto.org.cy

- Aristokyprou 11
  Laïki Geitonia
  CY 1011 Nicosia
  ☎ 2267 4264

- Spyrou Araouzou 15
  CY 3036 Limassol
  ☎ 2536 2756

- Georgiou A' 22
  CY 4040 Germasogeia
  ☎ 2532 3211

- Plateia Vasileos Pavlou
  CY 6023 Larnaka
  ☎ 2465 4322

- Gladstonos 3
  CY 8046 Pafos
  ☎ 2693 2841

- Leoforos Kryou Nerou 12
  CY 5330 Agia Napa
  ☎ 2372 1796

- CY 4820 Platres
  ☎ 25421316

- Vasileos Stasioikou 2
  CY Polis Chrysochous
  ☎ 2632 2468

North Cyprus
- Nicosia
  ☎ 227 2994 or 228
  8765Toilets

- Kyrenia
  ☎ 8152145 or 8152227

- Famagusta
  ☎ 3662864

OPENING HOURS REPUBLIC

○ Shops	● Archaeological Sites
● Offices	○ Museums
● Banks	○ Pharmacies

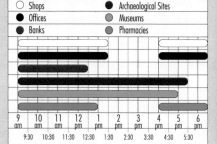

9 am	10 am	11 am	12 am	1 pm	2 pm	3 pm	4 pm	5 pm	6 pm
9:30	10:30	11:30	12:30	1:30	2:30	3:30	4:30	5:30	

In addition to the times above:
Republic of Cyprus Offices, shops and pharmacies close Wednesday and Saturday PM. Afternoon hours are 2:30–5:30 (offices 3–6) October to April. Banks open 8:15 July, August, Monday 3:15–4:45 all year. Banks in main tourist areas open afternoons. Most museums close for lunch and also one day a week.

OPENING HOURS NORTH

○ Shops	● Archaeological Sites
● Offices	○ Museums
● Banks	○ Pharmacies

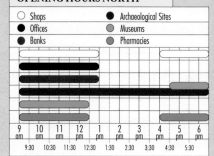

9 am	10 am	11 am	12 am	1 pm	2 pm	3 pm	4 pm	5 pm	6 pm
9:30	10:30	11:30	12:30	1:30	2:30	3:30	4:30	5:30	

In addition to the times above:
North Cyprus Shops and pharmacies open 8–1 and 2–6 in winter and shut Saturday pm in summer. In winter offices open 8–1 and 2–5; banks open 8–1 and 2–5; museums open 8–1 and 2:30–5.

ELECTRICITY

The power supply is: 240 volts

Square sockets, taking three-pin plugs (square-pin as in UK) are used. In older buildings, round two-pin sockets which take two-round-pin (continental-style) plugs are more common.

TIPS/GRATUITIES

Yes ✓ No ✗		
Restaurants (service is included)	✗	
Cafés (service is included)	✗	
Hotels (service is included)	✗	
Hairdressers	✓	50c/C£1
Taxis	✓	10%
Tour Guides	✓	50c/C£1
Cinema usherettes	✗	
Porters	✓	50p/bag
Cloakroom attendants	✓	50p
Toilets	✗	

PUBLIC TRANSPORT

Cross-Island Buses

Republic of Cyprus: Intercity and village buses operate frequently between towns and various holiday resorts with many trips per day. Almost all villages are connected by local buses to the nearest towns but services operate only on weekdays, once a day, leaving early in the morning, returning to the villages in the afternoon.
North Cyprus: Except for the main routes such as Nicosia to Kyrenia, buses are infrequent and do not run to a timetable; your fellow passengers are more likely to be soldiers than tourists.

Boat Trips

Republic of Cyprus: One-day boat excursions (including lunch) operate from May to October. Popular trips include: Limassol Harbour to Lady's Mile Beach; Pafos Harbour to Coral Bay and Pegeia; Agia Napa to Paralimni and Protaras coast; Larnaka Marina along Larnaka, Agia Napa and Protaras coast; and Latsi along the Akamas coast.
North Cyprus: From May to October there are boat trips (including lunch) from Kyrenia Harbour to the beaches at Acapulco or Mare Monte (☎ 8153708).

Urban Transport

Republic of Cyprus: Urban and suburban buses operate frequently only during the day (starting very early in the morning) between 5:30am and 7pm. During summer, in certain tourist areas, buses may operate until midnight. It is a good idea to check routes with your hotel.
North Cyprus: There is a good bus service within the main towns, with buses running approximately every half hour. Check with your hotel for more detailed information.

CAR RENTAL

Many firms, including the internationally known, though mainly local ones in the North. Cars are expensive in the Republic, less so in the North. Cars in both sectors bear distinctive red number plates starting with a 'Z' and are sometimes in poor condition.

TAXIS

In the Republic, service taxis, shared with other people (4 to 7 seats), operate between main towns every half hour. There are also rural taxis which operate in hill resorts and urban taxis in towns. In the North, taxis can only be found at taxi stands.

DRIVING

Speed limits on motorways and dual carriageways:
100kph; min 65kph (North Cyprus: 60mph)

Speed limits on country roads:
80kph (North Cyprus: 40mph)

Speed limits on urban roads:
50kph, or as signposted (North Cyprus: 30mph)

Must be worn in front seats at all times and in rear seats where fitted.

Random breath-testing. Never drive under the influence of alcohol.

Petrol in the north and Republic of Cyprus is cheaper than in much of Europe. Grades sold in the south are super, regular, unleaded and diesel. In the North unleaded petrol is not sold. Petrol stations in the south are open 6am to 6pm. with automatic credit card/cash vending at other times. In the North they may open until 9 or 10PM.

If you break down in the Republic of Cyprus 24-hour towing facilities are provided by the Cyprus Automobile Association in Nicosia (☎ 22313131), which is affiliated to the Alliance International de Tourisme (AIT).
If the car is hired, follow the instructions given in the documentation.

CONCESSIONS

Students
Cyprus is not really on the backpacker's route, but there are youth hostels in Nicosia, Larnaka, Pafos, Agia Napa and in the Troodos Mountains. For details contact: The Cyprus Youth Hostel Association, PO Box 21328, CY 1506 Nicosia ☎ 2267 0027; email: montis@logos.cy.net. The youth card 'Euro<26' secures discounts for ages 13–26 on a wide range of products; contact the Cyprus Youth Board, 62 Aglangia,Nicosia ☎ 2240 2600; email neolea@cytanet.com.cy.
Senior Citizens
Few concessions are made to elderly visitors. Most hotels offer discounts during the low tourist season, but you do not have to be a senior citizen to take advantage.

PHOTOGRAPHY

What to photograph: landscapes, picturesque villages, bustling towns, flowers and wildlife.
Restrictions: Near military camps or other military installations, in museums, and in churches with mural paintings and icons where flashlight is required.
Where to buy film: from shops and photo laboratories. Film should not be bought from kiosks as it may well have been 'roasted'.

PERSONAL SAFETY

The police are relaxed and helpful and English is widely spoken. In tourist areas in the south Cyprus Tourism Organisation representatives can provide a degree of assistance. However, crime in Cyprus is at a reassuringly low level. Any problem is more likely to come from visitors. Take the usual precautions with regard to handbags and valuables left in cars. Any thefts or offences should be reported to the police, if only for insurance purposes.

- Do not cross the Green Line (the dividing line between the two sectors) except on a day trip from Nicosia south to the north.

- Keep away from military zones (north or south).

- Do not use roads marked as blocked-off on a map (they may encroach on military zones).

Police assistance:
☎ **112** (Republic)

☎ **155** (North)
from any call box

TELEPHONES

In the Republic public telephones are found in town centres. They take 2, 5, 10 and 20-cent coins or *telecards* (C£3, C£5, C£10, from banks, post offices, tourist offices or kiosks). In the North public phones are scarce. They take tokens (*jetons*) or *telekarts*, sold at Telekomünikasyon offices.

International Dialling Codes	
From Cyprus to:	
UK:	00 44
Germany:	00 49
USA:	00 1
Netherlands:	00 31
Spain:	00 34

POST

Post Offices
There are main post offices in main towns and sub-post offices in the suburbs.
Republic Open: Mon–Fri 7:30–1:30 (Thu also 3–6)
Closed: Sat and Sun
North Open: Mon–Fri 8–1 and 2–5, Sat 8:30–12:30
Closed: Sun
☎ 22303219 (Republic)
☎ 2285982 (North)

HEALTH

Insurance
Tourists get free emergency medical treatment; other services must be paid for. For UK nationals benefits are available in the Republic by arrangement with the Department of Health before departure. Medical insurance is advised for all.

Dental Services
Dental treatment must be paid for by all visitors. Hotels can generally give recommendations for local dentists. Private medical insurance is strongly advised to all tourists to cover costs of dental treatment in Cyprus.

Sun Advice
Cyprus enjoys almost constant sunshine throughout the year. Wear a hat and drink plenty of fluids during the hot months (particularly July and August) to avoid the risk of sunstroke. A high-protection sunscreen is also recommended.

Drugs
Minor ailments can be dealt with at pharmacies (*farmakio* in the south, *eczane* in the North). Pharmacies sell all branded medicines. Some drugs available only on prescription in other countries are available over the counter in Cyprus.

Safe Water
Tap water in hotels, restaurants and public places is generally safe to drink though not very palatable in the North, particularly around Famagusta where the sea has invaded boreholes. Bottled water is cheap and widely available.

LANGUAGE

Cyprus has two official languages, Greek and Turkish. Greek is spoken in the Republic of Cyprus and Turkish in the North. Most Greek Cypriots speak good English but an attempt at the language is useful in, for example, the village coffee shop and similar places where locals may know no English. In the North things are different – not as much English is spoken. Waiters and others have only a limited fluency and some knowledge of Turkish is a definite advantage. Below is a list of some words that you may come across.

	English	Greek	Turkish
	hotel	xenodhohío	otel
	room	dhomátyo	oda
	...single/double	monó/dhipló	tek/iki kishilik
	breakfast	proinó	kahvalti
	toilet	twaléta	tuvalet
	bath	bányo	banyo
	shower	doos	dus
	balcony	balkóni	balkon
	bank	trápeza	banka
	exchange office	ghrafío sinalághmatos	kambiyo bürosu
	post office	tahidhromío	postane
	money	leftá	para
	cash desk	tamío	kasa
	credit card	pistotikí kárta	kredi karti
	traveller's cheque	taxidhyotikí epitayí	seyahat çeki
	exchange rate	isotimía	döviz kuru
	restaurant	estiatório	restoran
	café	kafenío	bar
	menu	menóo	menü
	lunch	yévma	ögle yemegi
	dinner	dhípno	aksam yemegi
	dessert	epidhórpyo	tatli
	waiter	garsóni	garson
	the bill	loghariazmós	hesap
	aeroplane	aeropláno	uçak
	airport	aerodhrómio	havaalani
	bus	leoforío	octobüs
	...station	stathmós	otogar
	boat	karávi	gemi, vapur
	...port	limáni	porto sarabi
	ticket	isitírio	bilet
	...single/return	apló metepistrofís	tek gidis/gidis dönüs
	yes	ne	evet
	no	óhi	hayir
	please	parakaló	lütfen
	thank you	efcharistó	tesekkür ederim
	hello	yásas, yásoo	merhaba
	goodbye	yásas, yásoo	hosça kal
	sorry	signómi	özür dilerim
	how much?	póso?	ne kadar?
	I (don't) understand	(dhen) katalavéno	sizi anliyorum

REMEMBER

- Contact the airport or airline 72 hours prior to leaving to ensure flight details are unchanged.

- Departure tax is included in the cost of an airline or ferry ticket in the southern Republic but in the North a tax of 1,000,000 Turkish lira is payable upon departure.

- Items of antiquity may not be taken out of Cyprus.

Index

TwinPack
Cyprus

Written and updated by Robert Bulmer
Edited, designed and produced by AA Publishing

A CIP catalogue record for this book is available from the British Library.

ISBN-10: 0 7495 4337 X
ISBN-13: 978 0 7495 4337 2

Material in this book may have appeared in other AA publications.

Published and distributed by AA Publishing, a trading name of Automobile Association Developments Limited, whose registered office is Fanum House, Basing View, Basingstoke, Hampshire, RG21 4EA. Registered number 1878835.

Colour separation by Keenes, Andover
Printed and bound by Times Publishing Limited, Malaysia

ACKNOWLEDGEMENTS
The Automobile Association wishes to thank the following photographers and libraries for their assistance in the preparation of this book:
CYPRUS MUSEUM 50; MARY EVANS PICTURE LIBRARY 39c, HULTON GETTY 9, MRI BANKERS' GUIDE TO FOREIGN CURRENCY 87.

The remaining pictures are held in the Association's own library (AA PHOTOLIBRARY) and were taken by A Kouprianoff, except:
M Birkitt F/Cover (f) cruiseboat, 12b, 12c, 13a, 13b, 14, 15, 18, 21, 22, 23b, 30b, 31a, 37a, 38a, 38b, 38c, 39a, 39b, 40b, 41b, 41c, 42a, 43b, 44a, 46b, 48a, 49b, 51, 53, 58, 61b, 90a;
R Bulmer 23a, 26a, 45a, 47a; S Day F/Cover (a) orchid, (b) Brandy sour drink, (c) Pachyammos church, (e) Statue; R Rainford 6, 7, 16, 36b, 37b, 43a, 54; H Ulucam 17, 27b.

A02811
Cover maps produced from mapping © Freytag-Berndt u. Artaria KG, 1231 Vienna-Austria
Fold-out map © Freytag-Berndt u. Artaria KG, 1231 Vienna-Austria

TITLES IN THE TWINPACK SERIES
• Algarve • Corfu • Costa Blanca • Costa del Sol • Cyprus • Gran Canaria •
• Lanzarote & Fuerteventura • Madeira • Mallorca • Malta & Gozo • Menorca • Tenerife •

Dear **TwinPack** Traveller

Your comments, opinions and recommendations are very important to us. So please help us to improve our travel guides by taking a few minutes to complete this simple questionnaire.

You do not need a stamp (unless posted outside the UK). If you do not want to cut this page from your guide, then photocopy it or write your answers on a plain sheet of paper.

Send to: **The Editor, AA TwinPack Travel Guides, FREEPOST SCE 4598, Basingstoke RG21 4GY.**

Your recommendations…

We always encourage readers' recommendations for restaurants, nightlife or shopping – if your recommendation is used in the next edition of the guide, we will send you a *FREE* **AA TwinPack Guide** of your choice. Please state below the establishment name, location and your reasons for recommending it.

_____

_____

_____

_____

Please send me **AA TwinPack**

Algarve ❑ Corfu ❑ Costa Blanca ❑ Costa del Sol ❑ Cyprus ❑
Gran Canaria ❑ Lanzarote & Fuerteventura ❑ Madeira ❑
Mallorca ❑ Malta & Gozo ❑ Menorca ❑ Tenerife ❑
(*please tick as appropriate*)

About this guide…

Which title did you buy?
AA *TwinPack* _____
Where did you buy it? _____
When? m m / y y

Why did you choose an AA *TwinPack* Guide? _____
_____
_____
_____
_____

Did this guide meet your expectations?
Exceeded ❑ Met all ❑ Met most ❑ Fell below ❑
Please give your reasons _____
_____
_____

continued on next page…

Were there any aspects of this guide that you particularly liked? _____

_____

_____

Is there anything we could have done better? _____

_____

_____

About you…

Name (*Mr/Mrs/Ms*) _____

    Address _____

_____

_____ Postcode _____

    Daytime tel no _____

Please only give us your mobile phone number if you wish to hear from us about other
products and services from the AA and partners by text or mms.

Which age group are you in?
    Under 25 ☐   25–34 ☐   35–44 ☐   45–54 ☐   55–64 ☐   65+ ☐

How many trips do you make a year?
    Less than one ☐   One ☐   Two ☐   Three or more ☐

Are you an AA member? Yes ☐   No ☐

About your trip…

When did you book? m m / y y   When did you travel? m m / y y

How long did you stay? _____

Was it for business or leisure? _____

Did you buy any other travel guides for your trip?
    If yes, which ones? _____

Thank you for taking the time to complete this questionnaire. Please send it to us as soon as
possible, and remember, you do not need a stamp (*unless posted outside the UK*).

Happy Holidays!